EDITORIAL

A new journal devoted to the subject of fortification through the ages reflects a growing interest in these often very conspicuous monuments of the past. It is an interest which in recent years has extended beyond the military landmarks of the Roman Empire and the castles of the Middle Ages to the defences erected by prehistoric man at one end of the time scale to the more recent survivals of the gunpowder artillery age, and to the physical traces of the Second World War. All have their own particular interest and fascination but collectively they have many elements in common. The needs of defence and responses to changing technologies produce timeless solutions as well as distinctive innovations.

No matter how regrettable the necessity for their existence might have been, there are many monuments in the landscape which demonstrate that permanent works of defence have long formed an essential part of man's

The eastern defences of the outer enceinte at Anarvarza, the first real capital of Armenian Cilicia. The fortifications of this little-known medieval kingdom are well documented in Robert W Edwards' book reviewed in this issue. *(Beaufort collection)*

cultural environment. They are a very visible element in the archaeology and history of much of the world. Simon Pepper in a recent review in the *Times Literary Supplement* (24–30 June 1988) wrote that 'Medieval Western Europe was studded with castles. As many as 14,000 have been listed for the German-speaking parts of the Continent, while conservative estimates for France, Italy, Spain and Britain place the probable grand total somewhere between 75,000 and 100,000.' This is a prodigious number especially when it represents a span of not much more than 500 years. The following 500 years has seen warfare on a far more intensive and extensive scale which, too, has left remains of its defensive works across the world.

Many individuals and specialist groups are increasingly studying the design, construction and use of fortifications of all ages together with subsequent developments,

1

whether in their own right or as part of a wider historical perspective. This journal intends to make their work better known to both the general reader as well as the specialist, through individual articles summarising current work and thinking, by lists and reviews of books and periodical literature, and by giving news of conferences and their discussions.

There are several international groups of scholars concerned with specific aspects of fortress studies and which, in their respective fields, act as focal points for discussion and publication. They include the International Congress of Roman Frontier Studies which meets every three or four years. Its 15th congress will be held this year at Canterbury, Kent, 2–9 September 1989. The last occasion when the Congress met in Britain was in 1979 at Stirling and its excursions featured the Antonine Wall. The opening article in this first issue of *Fortress* is Stephen Johnson's review of the results of recent archaeological work on Hadrian's Wall, and is therefore a particularly appropriate and timely contribution.

Christine Mahany's account of the 14th Chateau-Gaillard Conference of European Castle Studies, held in south-west France in September 1988, explains the origin and character of this international gathering which meets every two years. She provides an appreciation of the papers discussed and a description of the castles studied during the conference in the region of Najac, Aveyron. In subsequent issues of this journal there will be articles relating to the International Castles Institute, or IBI as it is known from its German title, whose interests range beyond medieval castles or *places fortes* to country house architecture on the one hand and to eighteenth century artillery fortification on the other. The youngest of these organisations is the Fortress Study Group which has its origins in the United Kingdom and specialises in artillery fortification up to recent times. The contents of the 1988 volume of its annual journal, *Fort*, is included in the publications listings elsewhere in this issue.

There are, besides, several national societies devoted to particular aspects of fortification. They include the Stichting Menno van Coehoorn of the Netherlands, the Simon Stevinstichting of Belgium, the Vauban Society of France, the Deutsche Gesellschaft für Festungsforschung e V (West Germany) and CAMP (Council on America's Military past). These are all concerned with artillery works. National societies interested in medieval castles are more numerous. They include Asociacion Española de Amigos de los Castillos, and the Instituto Italiano dei Castelli. In Britain, the newly formed Castles Study Group holds its annual conference in Glasgow in April 1989. It does not, at present, have its own publication.

The publications of other general or period-orientated archaeological societies contain much material relating to fortification studies, and these as well as more specific books and monographs will be brought to the notice of readers of this journal. It is not the intention of *Fortress* to compete or conflict with the objectives of other bodies but rather to make their work more widely known.

As well as attempting to keep abreast of current ideas, *Fortress* will also be concerned with the survival and protection of fortifications as part of the wider cultural heritage. It will be interested in ways of conserving fortifications as historical monuments and with their accessibility and greater understanding. This is of great importance since the remains of fortifications, while often having easy appeal to the general public, also bring out the destructive urges of the vandal.

The aim of the first few issues of *Fortress* will be to explore the range of fortifications across time and space, from prehistory to the present day, and across the world. Later, it is hoped that certain issues will concentrate on particular themes. These will involve the wider implications of defences: the subsidiary aspects of fortified areas such as weapon and munitions storage and supply, garrison requirements and the effects of fortifications on the inhabitants, siegework and its countermeasures, early warning systems, fire control and integrated defence systems, and, where they are known, biographical material relating to those involved with the fortifications. Potential contributors on these, or any other fortress subject, should write to the editor.

As a journal devoted to both the specialist and the non-specialist, it is intended that *Fortress* should present an opportunity for continuing dialogue and correspondence, inquiry and argument. So besides producing varied and, we hope, stimulating contents, we look forward to receiving and publishing your letters.

Andrew Saunders

RECENT WORK ON HADRIAN'S WALL

DR STEPHEN JOHNSON SURVEYS SOME OF THE REMARKABLE DISCOVERIES MADE ON AND AROUND THE MOST FAMOUS OF ROMAN FRONTIER DEFENCES. IN ITS HEYDAY, FOR EXAMPLE, THE WALL MAY HAVE BEEN FINISHED IN GLEAMING WHITE – A SUPERB VISIBLE SYMBOL OF THE BOUNDARY OF ROMAN CIVILISATION

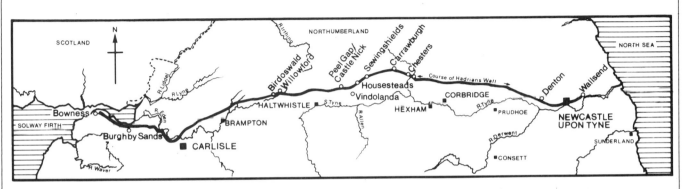

Map of Hadrian's Wall to show sites mentioned in the text.

At its fullest extent at the time of the emperor Trajan, the Roman empire incorporated not only the territories which fringed the entire Mediterranean Sea but considerable tracts of land well away from its immediate area. Trajan himself spent much time campaigning in the Near East, and incorporated Dacia (modern Romania) into a province whilst maintaining a hold on other Danubian and German provinces. Britain, whose amalgamation into the Roman world was begun in 43 AD, lay even further on the fringes of this world.

Internal security within an area so vast could not be guaranteed without constant watchfulness by the army on the borders. This does not mean to say that there was constant or sustained pressure by 'barbarians' from without; it was, however, important that Rome's links through trade, diplomacy and, on occasion, subsidy, maintained a stable equilibrium on border lands both inside and outside the formal 'frontier' area. Studies of the interaction of Romans and outsiders at the edges of the empire have long held scholars' attention, and since 1949 a series of international congresses of Roman Frontier Studies have been held to enable those whose experience of the Roman military presence lies in many parts of the empire to discuss themes of common interest.

In September 1989, the Congress comes again to Britain, and, just before it, the decennial pilgrimage along Hadrian's Wall, one of the most famous of Roman frontiers, is due to take place. It is perhaps ironic that Britain, so peripheral to the main focus of the Roman Mediterranean world, should contain the frontier system which is so renowned, and which bears Hadrian's name. This series of frontier works has now been added to UNESCO's World Heritage List, but it is still a monument which is being actively studied and is continually providing new information and evidence to enhance modern-day understanding and interpretation.

Hadrian's Wall stretches 80 Roman miles (about 73 statute miles or 117km) across the full width of England, from the River Tyne at Newcastle to the Solway Firth, west of Carlisle. Built in the years following 122 AD, and occupied by Roman troops in a virtually unbroken sequence until the end of the fourth century, it comprises a number of complex and substantial archaeological monuments. The Wall itself is studded with buildings: at every Roman mile there is a small fortlet ('milecastle') which allowed access through the curtain wall: equally spaced between each fortlet, there are two further towers ('turrets'). In addition, sixteen permanent forts lie either on or in close association with the Wall; the *vici*, or settlements, which grew round them are extensive. The curtain wall was the primary barrier but it was of stone only for the easternmost 49 miles or so, from Wallsend on the River Tyne to the crossing of the River Irthing at Willowford. West of that point, to the point where it terminated at Bowness on Solway, it was built originally of laid turves. Milecastles on this stretch of the Wall, and apparently some of its associated forts too, were also of turf, though these, like Hadrian's Wall itself, were later converted to stone. Throughout its length, the Wall was protected to its north where necessary by a ditch, and, to the south, by an earthwork known today as the *vallum* – a ditch between two banks – which runs almost the full length of the Wall's course across England.

Archaeological work on the Wall, aimed at a better understanding of its remains, has been intensive in this century, and in recent years much that is new has come to light. Sometimes this has been the product of new work aimed at specific problems or areas of research, while on other occasions new evidence has been found as a result of necessary recording or excavation in advance of a programme of works or repairs which would affect the Wall's remains. More than once, too, the new information was the result of sheer chance, when the unexpected turned up in construction work on the Wall's line. Even 'sheer chance', however, does not just happen: there must be the right people on hand to interpret what is being uncovered and to grasp the significance of the find.

THE CONSTRUCTION AND APPEARANCE OF THE WALL

The Wall's course across the country from the Tyne to the Solway Firth is clearly enough marked, but there are gaps in our knowledge in parts of the conurbations of Newcastle and Carlisle. Work on a new Arts Centre in Newcastle which lies on the known line of the Wall revealed that all trace of the Wall itself had been obliterated by the cellars of later buildings. In the courtyard south of the building's frontage, however, the remains of a milecastle were revealed, in a spot which does not readily square with the spacing of other similar structures. Elsewhere on the Wall's line, milecastles are regularly spaced, at about a Roman

mile (about 1650yds or 1500m) apart: the discovery of this milecastle close to the point which must have been the east end of the Wall – it was only slightly later extended a further 4 miles eastwards to Wallsend – poses new problems about its original layout. Did the Wall originally start from the Hadrianic bridge across the Tyne, or from some other point on the river's north bank?

Elsewhere, examination in detail of the curtain wall has revealed more that is new. In an area of Denton, west of central Newcastle, affected by construction work for a new city ring road, it was revealed that a fallen section of wall had once had a rendered mortar face, and must therefore in antiquity have presented a far different aspect from that of today. In excavations carried out in the Castle Nick area, further evidence emerged for the way in which the Wall was finished. In among the rubble of the upper portions of the barrier was stone from a chamfered string course which bore unmistakeable traces of white limewash on what must have been one of its exposed outer faces. It is possible, therefore, that the Wall was finished in a variety of ways, but could have been coated in gleaming white.

Part of the same programme of excavation and consolidation of the remains carried out in response to the problems of erosion by visitors on this highly picturesque area of the Wall also revealed fresh information about the sequence of its construction programme. Throughout its length, the Wall appears to have been completed in a number of different widths: Hadrian's original barrier appears to have been about 10 Roman feet (9.7ft or 2.96m) wide, and a number of other, narrower, gauges have normally been assigned to various phases of rebuild at later periods. Near milecastle 39, at Castle Nick, however, a stretch of wall foundation of 'Hadrianic' gauge was found which seems never to have had a superstructure built on it. What is more, when the Wall was eventually built in this area, it was not only to a narrower gauge, but on a different line, some 4–5m away from the Hadrianic foundation. At other points in the same area, there were indications of the presence of at least two separate phases of narrower wall than the original layout, the earlier probably of Hadrian's time, but the later perhaps part of an extensive rebuilding programme set in train by the emperor Septimius Severus around the year 200 AD. There were even suggestions that some portions of Hadrian's Wall may never even have got beyond the foundation stage at all, and may have been first built under Severus nearly 80 years later.

In Peel Gap, as part of the same campaign of work, a further surprise was in store. Normally each 'Wall mile' between milecastles contains two equally-spaced watchtowers, or turrets. Excavation of the curtain wall at the foot of Peel Crags, however, revealed that at this point there was a Roman tower attached to the Wall, making the third 'turret' between the adjacent milecastles. It differed from other turrets: it was not bonded to the wall, nor recessed into its thickness, and apparently of inferior construction. In addition, a platform or ramp – for access to upper storeys – lay outside its west wall. The presence of this additional turret shows yet again that the planning for the Wall was not as methodical or as automatic as is sometimes assumed. This, together with archaeological evidence for interruptions in the wall-building programme shows the value of detailed study of the remains.

Part of the programme of conservation in the Peel Gap area incorporated the excavation of milecastle 39, at Castle Nick. In its earliest phases, there was a long barrack block on the west side of the milecastle, with a series of smaller buildings on the east of the central roadway. Later modifications resulted in the provision of a pair of rectangular buildings opposite each other, with small porches leading off the roadway. A similar sequence was found at another of the milecastles, Sewingshields, suggesting that the period during which some of these were occupied was a long one.

The western end of the Wall was originally built of turf, and only converted later to stone. The opportunity has recently arisen to examine two elements of the curtain wall in this area. Near Burgh-by-Sands, west of Carlisle, the proposal to lay new pipes across the Wall's line to a sewerage treatment works made it necessary to examine the portion of the Wall and vallum affected by the scheme. It was found that the turf wall had been laid on a foundation of cobbles about 7m (23ft) wide, and that when the stone wall was later built, it was placed near the front of the turf wall's

Hadrian's Wall (right) and the attached tower in Peel Gap from the east. *(National Trust)*

line, and squarely planted on the cobbled foundation. The existence of the cobbled base for the turf wall had never been proved before, though it has for long been known that the Antonine Wall, built in the 140s between the Forth and the Clyde, was planted on a similar base.

Birdoswald fort was built around 124–5 astride the turf wall, and the opportunity has been taken to institute a 4-year programme of analysis of portions of the surviving remains. The site is a complex one, for excavations around 50 years ago revealed that the fort has a number of phases of construction, still imperfectly understood, and was apparently preceded by a number of temporary camps, originally interpreted as accommodation for working parties of men engaged on Wall- or fort-building. Excavation has been planned to include the west gate of the fort where it may be possible to examine the relationship between the fort and the early layout of the turf wall. At precisely the point where the turf wall met the fort's west gate, the excavators found that the gatehouse seemed to incorporate an earlier stone-built structure. This may have been a separate building – perhaps a tower or a gateway, which was part of the original Wall, or may even have pre-dated it.

VINDOLANDA: THE COMMANDANT'S RECORDS

Hadrian's Wall was built in the 120s but was the crystallisation of a build-up of frontier policies in this northern zone over the previous 40 years. A number of sites in the area, normally on the Stanegate road a little to the south, are known to have been early fort-bases for Roman troops in the area. One of these is Vindolanda where a fort was established in the 80s or 90s. Deep underneath the present remains just outside the south-west corner of the later fort, excavations have located waterlogged deposits, and led to the discovery of substantial numbers of finds of leather, wood and other organic materials. They were found within and around a timber building which has been identified as the Commandant's house. The quality and quantity of this material gives a glimpse of what may have been lost at other sites where the conditions have not been so beneficial. There was a large amount of animal bone, wooden implements, and textiles. More than 200 shoes or portions of them, in various styles and sizes (some surprisingly small, and possibly for women or children rather than

troops) were found. These, together with a considerable amount of offcuts and other pieces show that the process of tanning had been undertaken nearby – perhaps in an internal workshop.

The most exciting finds of all, however, were those of wooden writing tablets. Although over 400 of these have now been found, not all have yet been deciphered, and some of them may never have borne any writing. They come from three separate deposits within the fort dating from the years 90–100, between 100 and 105, and then down to 120 AD, and appear to form an archive of official reports, records of supplies and stores issued or requested, as well as a series of letters, some of which are those written to the occupants of the fort and others apparently file-copies of those sent out. Among the historical pointers that the tablets give is the name of the provincial governor, Neratius Marcellus, who is known to have been governor of Britain between 101 and 103, as well as the name of the fort's commander at the time, the *praefectus cohortis* Flavius Cerialis. The tablets certainly mention the presence at Vindolanda of both the third and ninth cohort of Batavians, and it seems likely that the eighth cohort may have been there as well, probably between 100 and 105 AD.

The official reports include a long five-page report on payments made *ad sacrum* – to the regimental strong room – and a list of foods supplied at the fort for a brief period in June (the year is of course not known), which includes several different types of meat as well as barley, corn, wines, beer and goat's milk, and which therefore gives a great deal of evidence about the variety of the Roman soldier's diet.

Other documents are duty rosters, cash accounts – including one which appears to show 'returns to the fort', perhaps from the sale of surplus materials to outsiders – and records of supplies or stock issued. One of these gives a list of a number of wooden items (spare parts used in the manufacture of carts) being sent out from Vindolanda.

One official report, quite short, but enormously informative about the way the Romans considered their adversaries and about the constant danger that they were in, reads: '. . . the Britons are unprotected by armour. There are very many cavalry. The cavalry do not use swords nor do the wretched Britons take up fixed positions in order to throw their javelins.' From this alone, one can gather some of the frustrations of being posted on

duty in the north, where the enemy are light, mobile and refuse to fight in the Roman cavalry fashion.

Letters within the archive, like many other such documents, are hardly literary masterpieces. One, however, is of great interest since it serves to show quite vividly what Roman life was like in what must have been considered a military zone. It is a letter from Claudia Severa, probably the wife of the commander of a nearby fort, to Sulpicia Lepidina, who must have been the wife of Vindolanda's commandant, Flavius Cerialis. The letter invites Lepidina to her birthday celebration on 9 September and sends regards from her and ` her husband and her little son. The letter, part of it written apparently in Severa's own hand, conjures up a vivid picture of the social round of commandants' wives stuck in faraway Britain on military service, who, amid all the workaday concerns of camp life, could find the time to travel in what must have been fairly hostile terrain to celebrate a birthday.

THE FORT AT CARLISLE

Excavations in Carlisle have located elements of the turf-and-timber fort contemporary with this phase at Vindolanda. It is now clear that the fort lay, at least in part, underneath the medieval castle. A Roman timber gateway uncovered in 1977–9 can now be seen to have been its south entrance. The fort was built in the Flavian period around 80 AD; part of its south rampart, south gate and associated rampart-back buildings were examined. Attached to the rear of the gate tower was a large workshop built of wattles and stakes; next to this lay a ramp of turf and timber for access to the ramparts and a shed and breadovens. The road just within the fort walls was narrow, and led off an open area bounded by post-built structures.

In a second phase, around 100 AD, the workshop next to the gate was demolished, the ramp up to the rampart extended, and the buildings within the fort altered and ex-

Hadrian's Wall at Burgh-by-Sands. The spread of cobbles shows the width of the original Turf Wall, later replaced by the narrower stone wall best preserved to the lefthand side of the picture. *(English Heritage)*

Above: The high quality stonework found incorporated into the west wall of Birdoswald fort near the point of junction with the Turf Wall. Compare the quality of this masonry with the more normal Roman masonry styles in the Peel Gap photo. *(English Heritage)*

panded. A pit in one of the rooms, which had been open at the time of demolition, yielded writing tablets bearing ink on wood; these have not yet been read, but we now have the exciting prospect at Carlisle and Vindolanda of contemporary correspondence from two sites, which might even interrelate.

THE WALL BRIDGES

Not all the work on the Wall in recent years has been directed primarily at excavation, and one of the priorities has been to record in detail, often for the first time, structures which have been well known and visible for many years. In 1982–3, in advance of consolidation work, Chesters Bridge Abutment was fully drawn, cleared of the stones which do not belong to its structure, and a limited campaign of exploratory excavation undertaken.

It is clear from the existing remains that the bridge which carries Hadrian's Wall across the River Tyne is in two main phases. Excavation located the robbed remains of the east abutment of the first bridge and demonstrated that the distance between the abutment and easternmost river pier (incorporated in the later abutment) was c4.0m (13ft). If the spacing of the piers throughout the bridge was equal and its overall length was equivalent to that of its successor, the bridge would have had eight piers and an overall span between its abutments of 61m (200ft).

The alignment of the Broad Wall foundation as it approaches the bridge from the east suggests that it was built before the exact site of the bridge had been chosen, but the massive construction, the closely spaced piers and the fact that the piers between their cutwaters are of a width suitable to carry the Broad Wall suggest that the bridge was of stone, and effectively carried the solid curtain wall across the river.

The plan of the second bridge was recovered by the excavations in 1860–3 but recent work has produced more evidence for the form of its vanished superstructure. Its overall length between the abutments was 57.5m (188.5ft) and it was carried across the river on three substantial piers spaced 10.5m (34.5ft) apart. Study of the large collection of architectural fragments after their removal from the bridge provides the principal source

Artist's impression of the bridge carrying Hadrian's Wall across the Tyne at Chesters as rebuilt around 220 AD. *(Drawn by Frank Gardiner)*

of evidence for the existence of voussoirs and therefore stone arches. In particular, moulded cornice blocks were identified. These had grooves to take vertical parapet slabs, and at intervals the parapet was interrupted by columns, four of which are so far known from the site.

The tower behind the east abutment is the base of a gatehouse with an earth ramp leading up to it from the east. A primary hearth in the tower produced an archaeomagnetic date of 220 AD plus or minus 10 years.

At a later stage, the south wing of the eastern abutment was extended, and subsequently a water channel was built behind the abutment running through the base of the tower. It probably served a mill down-stream from the bridge; excavation of the interior of the tower produced no evidence that this was the site of the mill as has been previously suggested.

In the light of this work, the remains of Willowford Bridge, where the Wall crosses the River Irthing, were also surveyed and partially re-examined by excavation. The bridge appears to have had three main phases of construction initially in association with the Broad Wall and, similar to Chesters, there was a large abutment, which had been much damaged, probably by flooding in Roman times; only the southernmost tip of its wing-wall survived. This was associated with the Hadrianic bridge, the first river pier of which was also examined. Though nothing of this survived *in situ*, there were clear traces of where it had lain, and blocks with dovetailed cramp-holes, probably originally from these piers, were found in secondary use in several places. A voussoir and a springer of a stone arch were found re-used in the second bridge; this strongly suggests that the first bridge was of stone rather than timber.

This abutment seems to have been scoured away in the 140s, and a new bridge, incorporating a massive additional pier of masonry, began from a point further west. A new wing-wall was built, and a tower on the south side of the curtain wall was added. Occupation within this tower suggests that this bridge continued in use until the early third century, when it was again rebuilt. This was the first road bridge on the site; the others had carried only a wall-walk. An earth ramp carried the road up to the bridge.

In examining the point of reduction between Broad and Narrow Walls, it was revealed that the core of the Broad Wall had been stepped down so as to remain stable until the Narrow Wall curtain could be brought up

to it. A section drawn through this area suggests that by projecting the angle of the stepped-down core to the point where the recess occurs, the approximate height of Hadrian's Wall can be calculated as between 4.0 and 3.5m (13–11.5ft) to wall-walk level.

EARTHWORK REMAINS

The Wall-zone is as rich in earthwork remains – surface traces of buried structures – as it is in elements of the masonry of the Wall and its forts. Comprehensive surveys of the earthworks at Bewcastle, Housesteads and Carrawburgh have been carried out by the Royal Commission on Historical Monuments of England. At Carrawburgh, a fort added to the Wall lies across the line of the vallum, just west of the site of milecastle 31. The earthworks of the fort are clearly visible, although, apart from on the west, there is no indication of the complexity of the ditch systems.

West and south-west of the fort lie most of the known buildings within the *vicus*, including the mithraeum. The location of the bath-house, excavated in the 1870s, is not clearly defined in nineteenth century accounts, but must lie south-west of the fort, where there is a flattened plateau close enough to the stream to be fed by it. Due west of the fort, a set of six terraces appear to have been cut into the slope, parallel with the fort walls, and overlapping most of the ditches. Most significant, however, is that west of the fort, Carrawburgh was protected by a pair of twin banks rather than ditches, perhaps intended to be a late additional defence to the western side of the fort.

Outside the east wall at Housesteads there seems to be a similar sequence. The fragmentary defensive banks here were cut through by stone robbers seeking stone from the *vicus* buildings east of the fort. This survey has shown the astonishing richness and complexity of the earthwork remains outside the fort.

Major excavation campaigns within the last decade or so on the Wall have concentrated on three of its forts. Those at Housesteads and Wallsend were completed some years ago, and their results are being studied in preparation for a final publication of new evidence. Both sites have shown the complexity of the sequence of building and use of various buildings within Roman forts, and have demonstrated the wide diversity of types of buildings in use at different periods of the forts' life. Of particular interest has been the opportunity to study the late-Roman layout within the forts in the third and fourth centuries. By this time, the former regular barrack-blocks had been replaced by rows of small huts – apparently quite similar to beach-huts at the seaside – thus earning the nickname 'chalets' from their excavators. What transformation within the Roman army this might indicate is a matter for speculation. Were individual soldiers setting up home for wives and families within the fort in those separate chalets? And if there were now only 8 soldiers housed where there

Artist's impression of the barrack blocks in the north-east corner of Housesteads fort, showing the separate 'chalets' as constructed in the later third or fourth centuries. The fort ramparts, of stone backed with earth, are to left of the picture. *(Drawn by Frank Gardiner)*

had formerly been a whole *centuria* of 80 men, was the fort garrison really reduced to a tenth of its former (Hadrianic) strength?

THE SOUTH SHIELDS FORT

Away from the Wall itself, but closely related to it, work at South Shields fort has also been continuing. It has until now usually been considered that the stone phases at South Shields are Hadrianic in date, but excavations near the site of the west gate have revealed traces of a timber rampart or ramparts pre-dating the stone phases. In addition, there is evidence from separate parts of the site for at least two periods of timber buildings and streets of an apparently pre-Hadrianic data. Occupation may have begun under Agricola, in the 80s AD.

Detailed work on the site of the head-quarters building has revealed something of this complexity. The earliest phases were of timber, and a metalled road crossed the site. The first fully stone headquarters was built on the site of an earlier unfinished building. This was altered in the late second or early third century by the erection of a building in the forecourt, and by the removal of one of the rear dividing walls to form a smith's work-shop. In the Severan period the site was completely built over, by two granaries, formed by adaptation of the cross-hall and the fore-court. Later still, the whole headquarters was rebuilt and turned round for the fort extended further to the south.

The excavations have revealed more evidence for the layout of the Severan supply base. The double granary which had original-ly belonged to earlier forts was retained, but at least twenty-two new granaries were added, including the two formed out of the earlier Headquarters. The fort was extended south-wards, and this area may have contained accommodation for the unit in charge of the supply-base – part of the *Cohors V Gallorum*. Around 220 AD the fort was modified and barracks were built on the site of the granaries south-east of the *principia*. The north-west part of the fort was divided off by a new wall which ran off from the new *principia*, now facing south.

In 270 or later, a large courtyard residence was constructed in the south-east corner of the fort. At the same time, it seems, the divid-ing wall was removed, the *principia* altered, and the remaining granaries (apart from the one behind the *principia*) demolished or altered to serve new purposes. This may be connected with a further change of garrison –

to the *barcarii Tigrisensium*. Occupation appears to have continued throughout the fourth century.

In the area of the west gate, the original inner ditch was filled up with debris from the gate and walls, including roofing tiles and a merlon cap. Towards the end of the fourth century, the ditch was re-cut and extended across the causeway. The fill of this recent ditch contained much rubble from the gate, including a solid stone window-head painted with voussoirs. The southern arch of the gate was dismantled and replaced in timber, and a new road was laid down. Inhumation burials across its line mark its final abandonment.

At Birdoswald, in the same campaign of excavation which identified a building which may have been in existence prior to the con-struction of the west wall, evidence came to light for the end of the Roman occupation of the site. In examining the pair of stone gran-aries, probably those rebuilt, according to an inscription, in 205–8, it was found that the

The excavation of the Birdoswald granaries, showing in the foreground the areas of metalled roadway, with, in the background, the pair of granary buildings (elements of their flagged floors can be readily identified). The figures are standing on the sites of posts set into the foundation trench for the post-Roman building which overlay the north granary and the road. *(English Heritage)*

southern one had been modified during the course of its existence, perhaps to effect its conversion into living accommodation. Ventilation gaps in the sub-floor walls were filled in, and a new floor laid, on which there were traces of hearths and domestic occupation. Although the northern granary was found to have the same sequence of reflooring as its southern neighbour, there was no trace of occupation debris on the floor. This granary's walls, however, were largely removed, and their stubs used as sill-walls for a timber building supported on posts set into the tops of these walls; its floor was formed of a crazy paving of carefully laid re-used facing stones.

More surprising still was the discovery that there was an even later phase of rebuilding than this on the northern granary site. A timber-framed building, the walls set in shallow trenches and its roof supported on posts set on padstones, straddled the site of the north granary, and lay partly over the road to its north. Only the padstones and the cobbled floor surface associated with them were identified. Although there were few datable finds from this building, it seems likely that it belonged to the post-Roman period, though whether this counts as evidence of a continuity of occupation here into the fifth or sixth centuries remains uncertain.

◆

This account of some of the major discoveries in the Hadrian's Wall area in recent years is necessarily brief, but serves to show the changes and improvements in our understanding of the frontier as a result of recent work. The thrust of continuing research shows that the Wall is still capable of springing major surprises. Its investigation, by survey, analysis and excavation where necessary, can only serve to increase our appreciation and strengthen our determination to safeguard its remains, wherever practicable, from modern pressures which may affect it.

CRUSADER CASTLES: THE FIRST GENERATION

DR DENYS PRINGLE LOOKS AT RECENT ARCHAEOLOGICAL EVIDENCE RELATING TO THE FRANKISH OCCUPATION OF THE HOLY LAND, CONCENTRATING ON THE KINDS OF FORTIFICATIONS BUILT BY THE NEWCOMERS IN THE TWELFTH CENTURY KINGDOM OF JERUSALEM

The Old French version of William of Tyre's Chronicle relates how, in 1144, King Amaury founded the castle of Ibelin (Yibna) between Ramla and Ascalon:

> First of all they laid the foundations; then they made four towers. Stones were to be found in sufficiency in those places where there had formerly been fortresses, for, as they say, 'A castle destroyed in a castle half-remade'.

In fact, time and again Frankish sources describe the Crusaders making use of earlier building materials found on the sites where they chose to build their castles. In 1218, for example, when the Knights Templar began to dig a ditch across the peninsula on which their enormous castle of ᶜAtlit (Pilgrims' Castle) was soon to stand, Oliver of Cologne relates that they uncovered not only ancient walls, affording a ready supply of building stone, but also freshwater springs, and coins which they used to pay for some of the building work.

Such stories come as no surprise to anyone with experience of Palestinian archaeology. In a land where the usual material for construction for many centuries has been stone, it is indeed common to find masonry from one period being used again in later ones. In addition, the topography of much of the country is such that sites chosen for settlement in antiquity have also tended to be favoured in later periods. For the principal factors governing the choice of sites, such as security, the availability of water, and proximity to agricultural resources, have changed little, even though the culture of the inhabitant has.

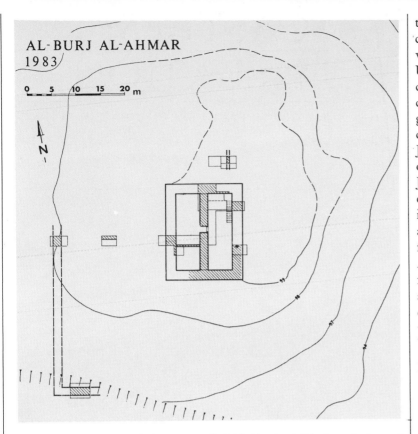

AL-BURJ AL-AHMAR
1983

0 5 10 15 20 m

N

The Red Tower (al-Burj al-
Ahmar): plan of the
castle as revealed by
excavation in 1983.
(Drawn by Peter E Leach)

Left: The Red Tower (al-
Burj al-Ahmar): south
wall of the keep, seen
from the north. *(Author)*

From one perspective, the foundation of the castle of Ibelin may therefore be seen as yet another example of the almost natural cycle of settlement-renewal. But looking at it from another angle, we may begin to wonder whether our medieval source is not leading us astray. It is true that the general pattern of settlement in the countryside of Palestine seems to have changed little with the advent of the Franks. If anything, the relatively stable conditions under Frankish rule in the twelfth century seem to have slowed down to some extent the progressive decline in rural population and agriculture, which had become particularly marked since late Byzantine and early Islamic times. But the new foundation at Ibelin was a castle; and though a small Frankish town, with its own Latin church and burgess court was later to develop beside it, it remained nonetheless an alien feature in the landscape, representing both physically and symbolically the imposition of a foreign military élite upon a largely peasant native population.

FORTIFICATION BEFORE THE FRANKS

The castles built by the Crusaders in Palestine were, from the start, rather different in design and purpose from the works of fortification that had existed there in the early Islamic period. Medieval Islam, like medieval Byzan-

tium, had (in theory at least) a more tightly centralized military system than there ever was in the West in this period. Under the Umayyad caliphs, in the seventh and eighth centuries, the palaces of the rulers had indeed combined defensive features with a high degree of domestic comfort. But in Palestine, castle-palaces such as Khirbat al-Mafjar, near Jericho, or Khirbat al-Minya, beside the Sea of Galilee, were a rarity to the west of the Jordan Rift Valley. Under the Abbasid caliphs, from the mid-eighth to tenth centuries, the coasts of Palestine were defended against Byzantine raids by a system of fortified towns (including Acre, Caesarea and Ascalon), forts and watchtowers; and fortified khans or caravanserais were also spaced along the main roads to ensure the security of communications within the state. But even in the eleventh century, when Palestine became a battleground between the Byzantines, Seljuks and Fatimids, few fortifications seem to have been erected apart from town defences, notably those of Jerusalem and Haifa.

In contrast to this record from the early Islamic period when, latterly at least, fortification seems to have been restricted almost entirely to the major towns, from Crusader times it is possible to document archaeologically over 100 fortified buildings other than town walls scattered throughout the Kingdom of Jerusalem alone; and a significant proportion of these (perhaps more than 50 per cent) seem to date to within three to four decades of the Crusaders' conquest in 1099.

THE FRANKISH DONJON

Unlike Muslim Palestine, by the end of the eleventh century in the West, castles were a common enough feature of the landscapes of France, western Germany, the Low Countries, England and Wales. Although still mostly of timber, some stone-built castles had also appeared. Such buildings represented both the fortified residences of local lords, knights and castellans, and also the military and administrative bases from which these men controlled the areas attached to them, on behalf of their feudal superiors – the greater barons, dukes, counts, the kings of France or England, or the German emperor. The word *donjon* (English, *dungeon*), which was applied to the massive tower, or keep, with which many such castles were endowed, represented in effect the physical expression of *dominium*, or 'lordship'.

Just how the lands conquered by the Crusaders in Palestine were first divided out amongst the conquerors is difficult to tell in detail, for few early charters have survived, and often we must rely simply on snippets of information contained in later grants or confirmations. Once a major lordship has been established, however, there is evidence for the granting of villages and their lands to individual knights, or groups of knights. And the existence in a number of villages so granted of early twelfth century towers or *donjons* suggests that these knights followed Western practice by building castles.

In the lordship of Caesarea, which King Baldwin I granted to Eustace Garnier sometime between 1101 and 1110, there is evidence for knights holding lands at the village of Qaqun (Caco) before 1110. From other sources we also know that a castle existed there by 1123; and in 1131 there is mention of a viscount, or castellan. At Madd ad-Dair (Montdidier), another village in the same lordship, the castle, with its central tower, was probably built before the death of Eustace Garnier in 1123, since it was he who donated the village to the Abbey of St Mary Latina in Jerusalem. Similarly, the castle known as the Red Tower (Burj al-Ahmar) was probably built either at the same time as Madd ad-Dair or at least during the lifetime of Eustace Garnier's successor, Walter I, who died between 1149 and 1154. Here the British School of

Karak in Transjordan, viewed from the south. The trapezoidal keep was added by the Muslims in the thirteenth century. (Author)

Left: Remains of a twelfth century Crusader tower at Yazur (Casale Balneorum, or Casel des Plains), forming part of a keep-and-bailey castle, which was refortified by the Templars in October 1191, occupied by Richard I of England in November 1191, and dismantled once again by Saladin in August 1192. (Author)

Archaeology In Jerusalem's excavations in 1983 revealed the foundations of a large *donjon*, measuring some 19.7m by 15.5m (64ft 7in × 50ft 10in) with a bailey wall some 60m (200ft) square enclosing it. Near by, at ʿUmm Khalid, in the outskirts of modern Nathanya, there is mention in 1135 of a castle (*castellaris*) belonging to Roger the Lombard, who also seems likely to have been a first-generation knight, in this case an Italian. And at Qalansuwa (Calansue), a surviving tower may perhaps represent the remains of the castle of Geoffrey of Flujeac, who was holding Qalansuwa indirectly from the lord of Caesarea in the 1120s, and who granted it to the Knights Hospitaller in April 1128.

These examples come from a fairly small area in the southern part of the lordship of Caesarea. When we look at the distribution of early castles and towers throughout the Kingdom, however, it seems that similar things were going on elsewhere. These early towers are unlikely to have stood alone. Often remains of other buildings still survive near them; and in a number of cases, as at the Red Tower, Burj Baitin (Bethel) north-east of Ramallah, Burj al-Farʿa north-east of Nablus

and Maldoim between Jerusalem and Jericho, the tower stood within an encircling wall in the manner of the keep-and-bailey castles of the West.

MORE COMPLEX FORMS OF CASTLE

Not all Crusader castles of the twelfth century, however, had a single major tower or keep. In 1132–3, while King Fulk was absent in Antioch, the Patriarch and citizens of Jerusalem began building a castle near Bait Nuba to protect pilgrims travelling between Lydda and Jerusalem from Egyptian raids. This castle, known as Castellum Arnaldi, is identified with the ruined village of Yalu. It was built on a spur between two valleys, overlooking to the north the Vale of Ayalon. It had an irregular outer enceinte, strengthened by large projecting rectangular towers.

The three principal surviving castles of the lordship of Transjordan were also without keeps. They are: Shaubak (Montreal), which Baldwin I established in 1115 with a garrison of knights and footsoldiers, and later granted to Romain of Le Puy; Karak, built on a natural spur by Payen the Butler in 1142 to

replace Shaubak as the principal castle of the lordship; and the castle in Wadi Musa (li Vaux Moysi), near Petra, built after Shaubak and before 1144.

Where the natural topography did not impose an irregular plan, we also find early twelfth century castles being built with regular, rectilinear layouts, and with rectangular corner- and interval-towers. One such was probably Ibelin itself, although there is very little now left of it. William of Tyre describes this as built on top of a hill 'of very strong masonry with deep foundations and four towers'. From William's description, it also seems that Blanchegarde (Tall as-Safi⁽ᶜ⁾), built the same year, was of this type. And the surviving remains of Bait Jibrin show that this castle, which William describes in 1136 as having an impregnable wall with towers, ramparts and a ditch, also had at its centre a rectangular enclosure with rectangular towers at the corners.

It has sometimes been observed that this type of castle has much in common with the design of late Roman or Byzantine forts. A more immediate prototype, however, existed nearer at hand in surviving early Muslim forts. The fort which survives on the sea shore at Minat al-Qal⁽ᶜ⁾a, the medieval port of Ashdod, is mentioned by al-Muqaddasī (c985) as a place where the Byzantines came by sea to ransom Christian prisoners. It has a trapezoidal plan, with solid cylindrical corner towers and intermediate buttresses along the outer faces of the walls, which possibly once supported machicolations. The gates are set in opposing walls between projecting semi-circular towers. Another similar example, also mentioned by al-Muqaddasī is Kafr Lam (Habonim), just south of Haifa. Both of these forts appear in Frankish sources (as Castellum Beroart and Cafarlet respectively), and Kafr Lam at least was reoccupied in the twelfth and thirteenth centuries. Architecturally, and probably historically, they may be associated with the series of ribats, or fortified Islamic convents, built along the North African coasts in the eighth and ninth centuries.

Some of the early twelfth century castles built by the Crusaders developed into larger, more elaborate complexes as time went on. Beaufort, for instance, which began life in 1139 as a fairly modest keep-and-bailey castle, had developed by 1268, when it fell to the Mamluk Sultan Baybars, into an extensive castle belonging to the Templars. At Majdal

Shaubak (Montreal) in Transjordan. Like Karak, a castle without a keep. *(Beaufort collection)*

Right: Interior of the tower at ar-Ram (Rama), showing the barrel-vaulted lower storey, the ground floor entrance, and remains of the staircase to the upper floors. *(Author)*

Yaba, the castle which Baldwin, Lord of Mirabel, held from Balian of Ibelin, Constable of Jaffa, in 1122 was also probably centred on a single residential tower, which despite having a Greek inscription over the door (looted from a Byzantine church of St Cyriacus, possibly the one recorded in Ramla in the tenth century), is closely comparable to other twelfth century examples. During the twelfth century, however, Mirabel developed into a significant fortress, which in August 1187 held out for several days against Saladin's mangonels. Survey by the British School in 1988 has revealed beneath the later Ottoman accretions a fairly regular castle plan, with a central courtyard surrounded by ranges of buildings (including the early tower), an outer wall with projecting rectangular towers well preserved on the west, and at the north a large oblong structure possibly forming a barbican.

NON-FEUDAL FORTIFICATIONS

Although some of the castles built by the Crusaders in the first half of the twelfth century developed in this way into more complex systems of fortification, most of them did not. Furthermore, a number of the villages (and their castles) which in the early years of the century had been granted to knights, we later find being brought together into the hands of a small group of major landowners – in particular, religious houses and the Military Orders. There seem to be two main reasons for these parallel developments. First, the Franks were always in a minority in Palestine; thus for security as well as for social reasons, they tended to congregate in the urban centres, rather than settle on the land. Secondly, it was a feature of the economic system in the Frankish East that fiefs did not have to be tied to land, as was usually the case in the West, but could be related to other sources of income: for example, to a proportion of the import duties levied in the port of Acre, or to the sale of water from a cistern. Even where a fief was related to lands, it was not necessary for the fief-holder to reside on them. Rents would simply be levied in kind from the villagers at harvest time; and even this operation was often done by native Christian or Muslim estate officials (in some cases the village headman) on behalf of the owner or tenant. Some of the smaller twelfth century castles and other rural buildings surviving in the countryside may indeed have been (or at least have become) the residences of such native officials; other castles may simply have been abandoned later in the twelfth century,

By the 1180s, therefore, larger castles were tending to be built and maintained only by the Military Orders and by the more important of the secular lords.

Some other factors also caused Frankish society in the East to develop rather differently to contemporary society in the West, and had an effect on the architectural evidence for Frankish settlement, including fortifications. Because of the hostile environment in which they were built, it was common in the East from late Roman times for religious houses outside towns to be fortified. The monastery of St Sabas, in the Kidron Valley, received its refuge-towers and a detachment of troops to defend it at the time of the Emperor Justinian, in the sixth century. These towers seem to have been rebuilt or at least strengthened in the twelfth century, when other Orthodox monasteries in the wilderness east of Jerusalem were also rebuilt and refortified.

Twelfth century Latin religious houses were also fortified. When Queen Melisende founded a convent for Benedictine nuns at Bethany in 1138, William of Tyre tells us:

> Since the place lay on the edge of the desert and thus might be exposed to the attacks of the enemy, the queen at great expense caused to be built a strongly fortified tower of hewn and polished stone. This was devoted to the necessary purpose of defence, that the maidens dedicated to God might have an impregnable fortress as a protection against the enemy. (XV 26: E A Babcock and A C Krey translation, *A History of Deeds Done Beyond the Seas*, New York 1943, II, 133)

In fact, the surviving remains at Bethany include not only a massive tower, 14.6m (48ft) square, dominating the site, but also a solid wall with projecting rectangular towers enclosing the two churches and the monastic buildings. Likewise, at Bethlehem, the twelfth century Frankish additions to the complex surrounding the Church of the Holy Nativity included an outer enclosure wall, with gateways on the west and south, and at the southeast corner a massive *donjon*, possibly containing the residence of the Bishop.

Another category of 'non-feudal' Frankish fortification resulted from the fact that there was in twelfth century Palestine no servile Frankish peasantry, such as existed in the West. The lower class of Franks remained freemen, and were legally defined as burgesses, the equivalent of town-dwellers in the West. Just as happened in the West in this period, attempts were made by various landowners to establish planned settlements, or

'new towns', in which building plots and lands were offered on attractive terms. One such was Magna Mahumeria (al-Bira), north of Jerusalem, where the canons of the Holy Sepulchre established a new town by 1115. In 1124, when the Egyptians from Ascalon raided the area, the old men, women and children of Mahumeria escaped almost certain death or enslavement by taking refuge in a tower, which Fulcher of Chartres records had only recently been built there. This tower may be identified as that around which there was later built the *curia*, or courthouse, of Mahumeria, where the canons' steward presided over the burgess court, and where the inhabitants were obliged to pay their rents and tithes. Another example of this kind of structure, which also began simply as a tower and enclosure wall, within which vaulted ranges were then built, is the same canons' *curia* at ar-Ram (Rama), another of their new towns north of Jerusalem. Physically these buildings were in effect little different from the keep-and-bailey castles exemplified by such buildings as the Red Tower; but they were not true castles, in the sense of being the residence of a feudal lord.

Such examples highlight some of the difficulties in trying to define the functions of Frankish rural buildings from their material remains alone. One particular class of semi-fortified rural building, whose function it is often impossible to determine without historical documentation, is illustrated by a building surviving at Khirbat Bir Zait, north of Ramallah. Here we find remains of vaulted ranges, as at Rama, set around a central courtyard. The building at ʿUmm Khalid was also of this type; but if it was indeed the castle built by Roger the Lombard, then here at least we would seem to have evidence of a feudal owner. This building also had a solid clasping buttress or turret at one of the corners. The same type of corner- and interval-buttresses or turrets are found on the inner ward of the complex at Burj Bardawil, north of Ramallah, where an early rectangular nucleus seems later to have expanded in a fan shape downhill to the north, the vaulted ranges following the contours of the slope. And at Jifna in the same area there is another unexplained courtyard complex in the village centre.

Courtyard buildings such as these are often referred to as 'manor houses', and are sometimes held to indicate the existence in the twelfth century of a class of non-feudal landowner, a sort of yeoman-burgess. This notion is hard to accept. Indeed, some recent surveys by the British School have shown two sup-

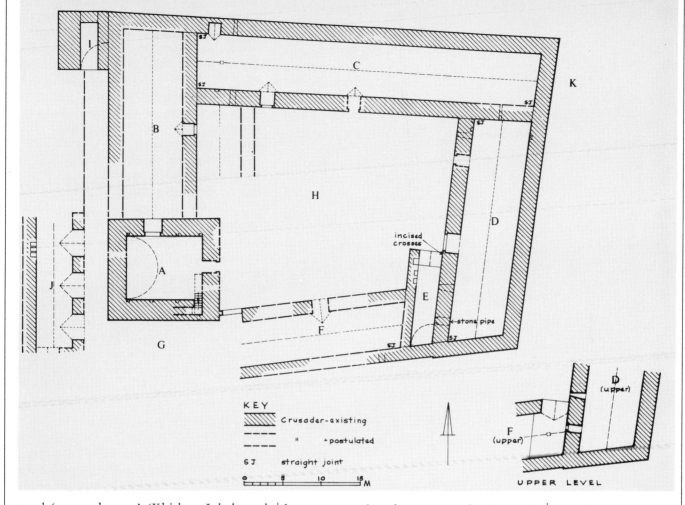

KEY

	Crusader-existing
- - - -	" - postulated
SJ	straight joint

UPPER LEVEL

posed 'manor houses' (Khirbat ʿIqbala and ʿAllar as-Sufla) to have been ecclesiastical buildings. Others were certainly secular. Some may well have had feudal owners or tenants and have been the Crusader equivalents of the *maisons fortes* – something between a house and a castle – found in the West. Others could easily have been the residences and storerooms of estate officials who administered the lands of absentee landlords.

BELMONT

Frankish settlement in, and exploitation of, the countryside seems to have been particularly intense in the area closest to Jerusalem. The largest establishment of the Knights of St John (Hospitallers) in this area, outside the city itself, was at Suba, some 10km to the west, where their castle of Belmont certainly stood by 1169, and possibly some two to three decades before that. In August 1187, Belmont fell to Saladin, and in September 1191 it was demolished by al-ʿAdil, Saladin's brother. As a castle, it therefore had a very short life, no more than half a century. The village of Suba,

however, continued to occupy the site until 1948.

Since 1986, Belmont has been the subject of a programme of excavation sponsored by the British School in Jerusalem and directed in the field by Richard P Harper. The castle is situated, as its name suggests, on the summit of a hill. Its outer walls describe an irregular octagon, following roughly the shape of the hill and measuring overall some 100m by 115m (330ft × 380ft) but with apparently no projecting towers. The walls are sloping, part masonry and part rock-cut, with a horizontal berm at their foot and no outer ditch. The outer gate, on the south-east, consisted of a double wing door, set in an irregular gatehouse; possibly there was also an outwork or barbican. Having entered this gate, however, the visitor, whether friend or foe, would have been confronted by yet another gate before he could get into the outer ward of the castle; the position of this second gate has yet to be determined, but it now seems likely that it would have been on the west or south-west. Where it has been examined on the south-east, the outer ward is defined by a continuous

Plan of the vaulted complex at ar-Ram, built to accommodate the steward of the canons of the Holy Sepulchre in the twelfth century. *(Drawn by Peter E Leach, from author's survey notes)*

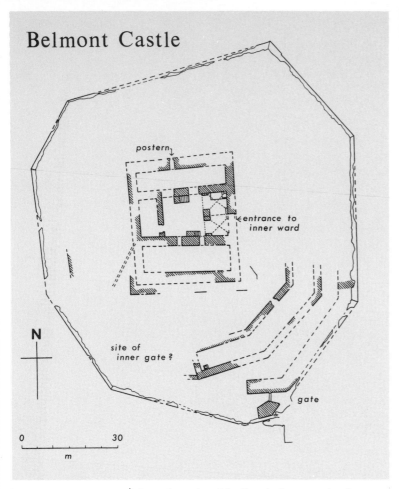

Belmont Castle

postern

entrance to inner ward

N

site of inner gate ?

gate

0   30
m

Plan of Belmont Castle
(Suba) as revealed by
excavation up to 1988.
*(Based on survey drawing
by Matthew Pease)*

and south sides of the courtyard respectively.

An obvious architectural comparison for Belmont is Belvoir, the great Hospitaller castle built from 1168 onwards just south of the Sea of Galilee, overlooking the Jordan Valley. This site too was covered by a village until 1948, but was cleared and excavated by the Israel National Parks Authority in the 1960s. At Belvoir, as at Belmont, there is a rectangular inner ward (some 50m or 104ft square), surrounded in this case by a rectangular outer one (100m by 110m, 328ft by 360ft); and in addition, there is a rock-cut ditch on three sides, and a barbican downhill on the fourth. But even allowing for the fact that Belvoir was built on a relatively flat site, and was not therefore constrained as much by the natural topography, its design seems more assured than Belmont's, as though its builders were working to a set plan from the start. In addition, both wards at Belvoir were also strengthened by projecting rectangular towers, and some of those on the outer walls had postern gates. Belmont, on the other hand, gives the impression of having developed in a more piecemeal way. The inner ward is comparable to the semi-fortified courtyard buildings described above; it may possibly even have begun its existence as one, only later being incorporated into a castle.

A much closer architectural parallel for Belmont is the Castle of St Elias in at-Taiyiba (Effraon), north-east of Ramallah. This had evidently been built sometime before 1185, when it was granted by Baldwin V, the child king, to his grandfather William of Montferrat. Like Belmont, its Crusading history ended abruptly in 1187. Here we find the same kind of polygonal outer wall, with a sloping face (*talus* or *glacis*). The inner ward is also similar, though more compact. It was roughly 28m (92ft) square, with solid clasping buttresses or turrets at the corners and midway along at least one of the sides. The gate, some 1.4m (4ft 7in) wide, led through a large barrel-vault, 6.6m (21ft 8in) wide, into a central open court of the same width, from which other vaults opened to north and south. Directly opposite the entrance, a smaller door (flanked by two windows) gave into another barrel-vault running the length of the building. The arrangement of the upper floor is unknown, since it has completely disappeared.

In a number of the concentric castles built by the Military Orders in the twelfth and thirteenth centuries, it is known that the chapel lay within the inner ward. This is the case at Templar Safad, ʿAtlit and Safitha

barrel-vault with slit windows and at least one large door opening from inside the castle, but no openings on the outside.

Within the outer ward, at the summit of the hill, stood a rectangular inner ward, some 32m by 38.5m (105ft × 126ft) overall. The main entrance to this seems to have been on the east, so that in order to reach it from the outer gates one had to follow a tortuous path, making almost a complete circuit of the castle, at all times being exposed to attack from the defenders on the wall-heads above.

In design, the inner ward is not at all unlike some of the courtyard buildings examined above. It seems to have consisted at first of three barrel-vaulted ranges, lying north, south and west of a central court. The east side of the court was built over at a later stage, with a pair of groin-vaults supported on rectangular piers. As in most other Crusader courtyard buildings, there are no properly developed projecting corner towers, though there is some indication of turrets or buttressing at the southern corners. The principal living areas, including the knights' dormitory, refectory and chapel, and the lodging of the castellan, would probably have been at the level of the first floor, which does not survive. There are in fact remains of two staircases on the north

Belvoir Castle

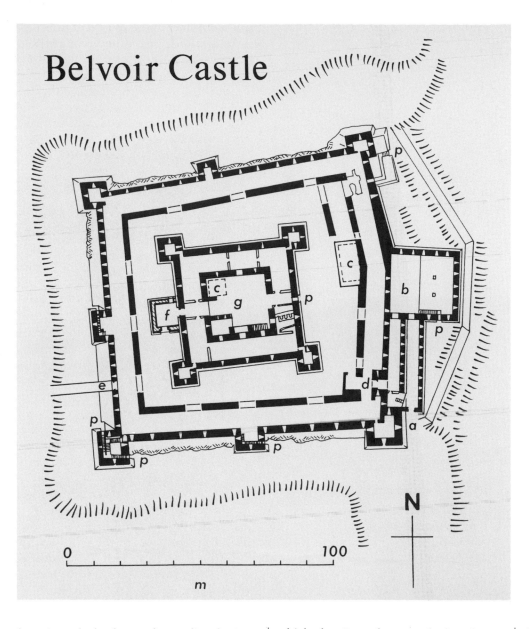

0   100
m

N

(where it took the form of an *église-donjon*), and at Hospitaller Marqab, Crac des Chevaliers and Belvoir (where it was over the gatehouse). It seems reasonable to assume therefore that in these castles the inner ward would have constituted in effect the monastic cloister of the brother-knights, and that the other, non-religious members of the garrison, such as the sergeants, mercenaries, and servants, would have been housed in the outer ward round about. It would be going too far, however, to suggest that concentric castles like Belvoir developed purely in response to the monastic needs of the Military Orders. For the concept of 'concentric' planning, with two lines of defence, one inside the other, both strengthened by projecting towers, had been current in the Mediterranean world since Hellenistic times, and is found, for example, in the very fortresses and town defences built by the Byzantines, Seljuks and Fatimids

which the Crusaders attacked and captured on the First Crusade and after. The twelfth century concentric castles of St Elias and Darum (Dair al-Balah), south of Gaza, were in any case royal castles, not apparently built by the Military Orders.

The function of castles was not simply to serve as garrison posts. A text relating to Safad, dating from the 1260s, places great emphasis on the economic benefits which accrued from the Templars' rebuilding of this castle from 1240 onwards. The presence of a garrison, prepared to take the field whenever the need arose, acted as a deterrent to Muslim raiding, and thus allowed the peasant agriculture of the region to develop once more. Castles also served as estate centres, in exactly the same way as some of the semi-fortified buildings described above. It seems likely, for instance, that one of the duties of the castellan of Belmont would have been to administer the

23

collection of rents and tithes from the Hospital's lands in the region. These would of course have included renders in kind; it is therefore no surprise to find inside castles evidence for agricultural processing, such as the wine-presses preserved at Belmont and at Montfort Castle in Galilee. Another source of evidence for agricultural produce being brought into castles, either to feed the garrison or for eventual sale, comes from the excavation of carbonized grain and animal bones. The British School's excavations at the Red Tower in 1983

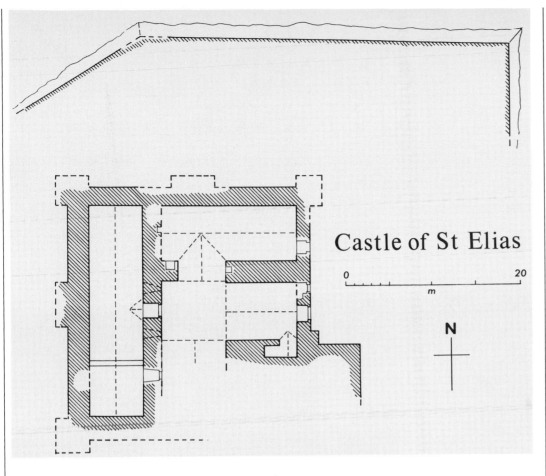

Plan of the Castle of St Elias (at-Taiyiba).
(Surveyed in 1988 by Matthew Pease and the author)

Castle of St Elias

0   20

m

N

produced evidence for a variety of crops, including broad beans, bread wheat, chick peas (*hummus*), two-row hulled barley, lentils and grass pea being cultivated, threshed and cleaned in the immediate vicinity. Preliminary analysis of the faunal material from Belmont by Dr Gillian Clarke has shown that, as at the Red Tower (and of course in the medieval West), the Franks seem to have been particularly fond of pork, which is almost completely absent from all other phases.

◆

Current work by the British School of Archaeology in Jerusalem is thus contributing to a broadening picture of the development of Crusader castles and of Frankish settlement in Palestine in the twelfth century. There is still much work to be done, in excavation, in field survey, and in the analysis of finds. Out of it all, however, it is hoped that we may eventually learn more about the construction of castles in the twelfth century, about the military and economic activities of castle-owners, particularly the Military Orders, and about the development of rural society, settlement and agricultural exploitation in Palestine during the Middle Ages.

Further Reading

M Benvenisti, *The Crusaders in the Holy Land* (Jerusalem 1970).

R P Harper and D Pringle, 'Belmont Castle: A Historical Notice and Preliminary Report of Excavations in 1986', *Levant* 20 (1988), pp101–118.

T E Lawrence, *Crusader Castles*, edited by D Pringle (Oxford 1988).

J Prawer, *The Latin Kingdom of Jerusalem: European Colonialism in the Middle Ages* (London 1972).

J Prawer, *Crusader Institutions* (Oxford 1980).

D Pringle, 'Two Medieval Villages North of Jerusalem', *Levant* 15 (1983), pp141–177

D Pringle, 'Magna Mahumeria (al-Bıra): The Archaeology of a Frankish New Town in Palestine', in *Crusade and Settlement*, edited by P Edbury (Cardiff 1985), pp147–165.

D Pringle, *The Red Tower (al-Burj al-Ahmar): Settlement in the Plain of Sharon at the Time of the Crusaders and Mamluks*, British School of Archaeology in Jerusalem, Monograph Series, 1 (London 1986).

R C Smail, *Crusading Warfare (1097–1193)*, Cambridge Studies in Medieval Life and Thought, No 3 (Cambridge 1956).

R C Smail, *The Crusaders in Syria and the Holy Land*, Ancient Peoples and Places Series, 82 (London 1973).

THE CHÂTEAU-GAILLARD CONFERENCE

ARGUABLY THE MOST PRESTIGIOUS EVENT IN THE CASTLE STUDIES CALENDAR IS THE CHÂTEAU-GAILLARD CONFERENCE. THE FOURTEENTH MEETING, AT NAJAC, AVEYRON IN FRANCE, WAS HELD BETWEEN 29 AUGUST AND 3 SEPTEMBER 1988 AND WAS ATTENDED BY CHRISTINE MAHANY, WHO DESCRIBES THE CONFERENCE AND ITS PROGRAMME OF VISITS TO THE MORE INTERESTING LOCAL CASTLES

The Château-Gaillard Conference takes its name from Richard Coeur-de-Lion's great castle on the Seine at Les Andelys, surely one of the most beautiful and impressive fortresses in western Europe. This was the venue chosen for the first conference of students of *castellologie* in 1962, which owed its inspiration very largely to the doyen of French medieval studies, Michel de Boüard, who remains the President. Although the Conference *Proceedings* are now published under the imprint of the University of Caen, the conference is truly international in flavour and peripatetic in character. Meeting every two years with attendance by invitation, it travels on a rotational basis to most of the countries in north-western Europe where castles are to be found: France, Germany, Switzerland, and England; and to some where the scale of fortification is generally but not always, more modest, like Holland, Belgium, and Denmark.

Although the title page of the *Proceedings* describes the contents as 'Studies in Castellology' the Château-Gaillard Conference is a very broad church, and papers have addressed a wide range of peripheral topics, and a no less wide range of topics to which strict 'castellologie' is peripheral. This is surely as it should be, although, as with most such gatherings, one might query the occasional contribution. This year, for example, people have wondered whether the excavation of the site of a post-medieval gallows, interesting perhaps in palaeo-medical terms, was close enough to 'the sub-title' to justify inclusion. On the other hand, contributions, which could hardly be fitted into the strict canon of castle studies either, were welcomed for the stimu-

lus which they offered, or the degree to which they broadened the mind.

From time to time there have been efforts to impose or suggest a thematic framework to the papers for any given year, but on the whole delegates have wanted to speak on subjects dear to their own hearts, namely, the results of their own research. These have ranged from detailed studies of the 'I dug this hole here' or 'regardez cette meurtrière là' kind, to regional studies embracing whole countries. The first approach obviously depends heavily on the quality of the excavation, and/or the distinction or interest of the monument or site examined, the second on the degree to which the fortifications of a region are known and understood. Contributions which combine synthesis with detailed scholarship are perhaps the most illuminating of all.

Side by side with the papers, which come in the three conference languages (English, French, and German) are the excursions to fortifications in the region where the conference is held. Often the monuments visited are little known, or imperfectly understood, and the opportunity to examine, discuss, and argue about them is valuable for delegates and hosts alike. Some countries are rather shy about showing monuments in a state of decrepitude, and some go to the other extreme of rebuilding them. The care and conservation of standing monuments is a very sensitive subject, and countries have very differing ideals and resources. The fact is, though, that many distinguished monuments in Europe have suffered grievously either from over-restoration, or from no conservation at all. The happy medium of 'conserve as found', is desirable but not always desired, and certainly is rather infrequently attained.

Not the least useful and enjoyable aspect of the Château-Gaillard conferences is the chance to exchange ideas with old friends. Host countries vie with each other in the quality of their hospitality and entertainment, and there have been some very memorable evenings over the years. It will be a long time before anyone forgets the hospitality of Lord Home at The Hirsel in 1980, or the barbeque in the woods above Münstereifel in 1976. No less memorable in its way will be the Soirée Folklorique at Najac in 1988, with 'troubador' songs and Occitan bagpipes.

The last French Château-Gaillard conference had been in 1974, at Blois, so for various reasons the Najac conference was eagerly anticipated, and carried the added frisson that,

Left:
The castle of Najac from the south-west. The medieval town is below it, and the church is to the left. (R A Brown)

Below: Najac. The castle seen from the axlal road of the later medieval town. (Author)

numbers being strictly limited, there had to be a ballot for places. One can only sympathise with those who drew the short straw.

Najac is an impressive site by any standards. The great castle and its little town rise above the valley of the Aveyron, a tributary of the Tarn. The river cuts a winding gorge through the predominantly limestone 'causses', which here have thickly wooded slopes. Above the river valley there are stupendous views towards Cahors to the north-west, the foothills of the Auvergne to the north-east, and the plains of Languedoc to the south. The history of the region is complex. Rouergue, wherein Najac lies, is called 'la basse Marche', and has been subject to a variety of influences. It was fought over almost continuously throughout the Middle Ages, and since. It looks west towards English Gascony, and its rivers flow through Bordeaux, but politically it had closer affinities with the south and east, towards Languedoc, the county of Toulouse, and the Mediterranean. From this direction, from Lombardy, came the gnostic philosophies of the Cathars, which, allied with Languedocian regionalism, provoked the painful episode of the Albigensian Crusade. Rouergue effectively formed a buffer zone between the realm of France and the heretical Albigeois. Many towns in the Midi, or within the orbit of the county of Toulouse, had Cathar sympathies, but the Crusade had as much political as religious motivation, in providing an opportunity for the French King to extend his influence over the separatist south, and at the same time isolate Gascony. Problems between English and French interests in the south-west continued throughout the thirteenth and early fourteenth centuries, culminating in the

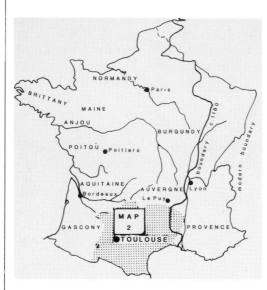

Map showing the County of Toulouse in c1180. (Author)

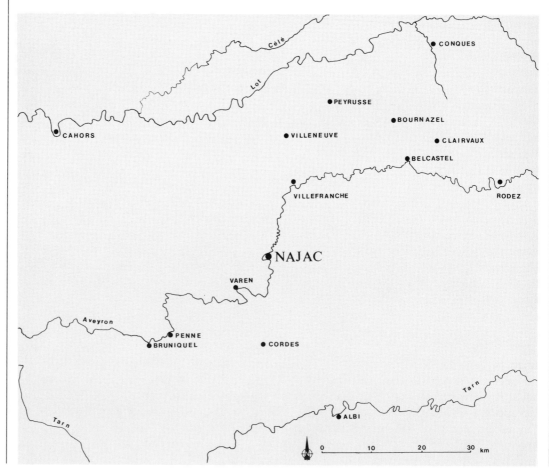

Map showing Najac, in the Rouergue region, and the sites visited. (Author)

Hundred Years' War, when Rouergue was overrun for a time by the armies of the Black Prince. The Wars of Religion, in the sixteenth century, resulted in the damage or destruction of many of the area's towns and castles. A town like Cordes seemed to have an uncanny knack of backing the wrong horse, and was repeatedly ravaged. Not surprisingly, the region is rich in castles, and in defensible churches; also in new towns, or 'bastides'. This was indeed a society prepared for war, and the physical evidence of this is all around to be seen. The castles of the region tend to be sited on rocky eminences along the river valleys. Most have antecedents going back into the eleventh or twelfth centuries, but were rebuilt and enlarged in the thirteenth century. Many suffered multiple changes of lordship, and most were occupied at one time or another by the English.

THE CASTLES OF ROUERGUE

Najac, perhaps the finest and strongest castle in Rouergue, is perched on a rocky hill of gneiss. It is large, impressive, and disciplined in its appearance, and has something of majesty in its domination of the little town, and of the region. This is to be expected in considering that it was chiefly erected in its present form by the last Count of Toulouse, Alphonse of Poitiers, brother of King Louis IX of France. The castle consists of a rectangular inner ward incorporating round towers at three corners, and an earlier square twelfth century donjon at the fourth. One of the round towers, larger than the others, contains vaulted rooms, and acts as a donjon. There are two intermediate towers in the long sides of the rectangle. Formerly there were buildings within it, as there were on an enclosed apron to the east. The whole is enclosed within an outer polygonal enceinte, incorporating two square towers and a gate. The village associated with the twelfth century castle lay just below it, huddled on a steep slope, near the existing thirteenth century church. On an adjacent hill, and joined to the castle by a narrow neck of land, stretches the axial road of the later medieval town, and its large market place, with some houses projecting over the pavement at first-floor level, supported on pillars.

The seigneurial history of Najac is typical of towns and castles in the region. It fell under English influence in the late twelfth century, through Henry II's ambitions as Duke of Aquitaine to contest the powers of the Count of Toulouse. But a marriage between the

Najac. The castle showing the twelfth century donjon. *(Author)*

Count and the king's daughter brought Najac again into the Count's domain. In the religious struggles of the Albigeois, successive Counts played an equivocal role, at one time supporting Languedoc and the Cathars, and at another conceding allegiance to the king of France. Towns like Najac were used as political footballs, now on one side, now on another, reflecting the count's current alliances. However, in 1229, Count Raymond VII entered into a dynastic arrangement, through his daughter, with Alphonse of Poitiers. This was an immensely significant development, for when Alphonse came into his wife's inheritance in 1249, on the death of Raymond VII, it brought the County of Toulouse into the realm of France, and ended the separatism of the Midi. Alphonse was initially unpopular, and a minor rebellion took place in Najac, causing damage to buildings and property. Reprisals followed, the populace submitted, and a conspirator was burned as a heretic. But by 1255, Alphonse is seen granting a charter to the inhabitants confirming their traditional customs and usages. To discourage further insurrections, and perhaps with an eye to future problems with the English, Alphonse rebuilt the castle, and it is his work which chiefly remains. Najac played a small part in the Hundred Years War. Its fortifications were repaired when the English penetrated the region in 1351, and it was put in readiness for a siege. In 1356, Najac was ceded to the English, but in 1370, they left Rouergue, and the castle declined in importance. Apart from the odd ugly incident, the Hundred Years War had passed relatively smoothly.

Penne is another of Alphonse of Poitier's great castles. This lours even more precipitously over the Aveyron, downstream from Najac. Unhappily it is in a sad state of preservation, and very much overgrown. It had also been badly damaged in 1588 in the Wars of Religion. Penne received its first recorded mention at the beginning of the eleventh century, but most of the surviving fabric was built by Alphonse, perhaps by the same hands as his work at Najac. The castle is difficult to understand without a plan, but there is a round tower, a gatehouse with a tower *en bec*, and several internal buildings, including a vaulted room. The ancient and picturesque walled village, divided into two parts by the porte Méjane, stretches along a single street and lies at the foot of the rock upon which the castle stands.

Not far from Penne lies **Bruniquel**, overlooking the confluence of the Aveyron and the Vère. It controlled the toll on the route from Cahors to the Albigeois. Like most of the castles in the region the earliest mention occurs in the late eleventh century, but the surviving parts are more recent. The original castle was probably smaller than that which survives, its defences running from the cliff edge to the existing small square twelfth century donjon. The castle consists of two independent but adjacent elements, the partition dating to 1461. The 'old' castle contains the donjon and a fine medieval two-storied hall, restored in the nineteenth century, and later buildings. The 'new' castle is of the late fifteenth and sixteenth century, with later additions and exterior adaptations for the use of guns in the seventeenth century. A programme of restoration is contemplated. The present enceinte which surrounds both the 'old' and the 'new' castle carries, not flanking towers, but rectangular buttresses, apparently in connection with hourds. A ditch separated the castle from the small walled town, the defences of which were enlarged in 1355 to include the suburbs. The enclosure of the 'faubourg' within an additional enceinte is also seen at Cordes and Peyrusse and reflects the growing importance of the bourgeousie.

In the canton of Rignac, higher up the Aveyon is the castle of **Belcastel**, first mentioned in 1040. Of this period only the chapel remains. The castle, which has an uncertain future, has been over-restored in recent years by private hands. Constructed on a rock, the castle dominates the river, village, bridge and small church on the opposite bank. To the north and west it is protected by a deep artificial ravine. The irregular enceinte followed the form of the rock, and was flanked by five large and four small round towers. The domestic building enclose a square donjon. Access to the courtyard was by a drawbridge, of which traces remain. Belcastel is typical of the castles of minor lords in upland areas, whether it might be in France, Switzerland or Wales. It has a limited rocky terrain which dictates the form of the enceinte. The same characteristics are found in the Cathar castles surrounding Carcassonne.

One of the most complex and interesting fortifications of Aveyron is at **Peyrusse**, the centre of an ancient *balliage* which extended its jurisdiction over 107 parishes towards Conques and Rodez. The site itself has possible Gallo-Roman antecedents and 'Petrucia' receives a mention in a document of 767, in the time of Pepin the Short. In the thirteenth century Peyrusse passed from the suzerainty of the counts of Rouergue into that of the king of France. Its '*floruit*' was clearly in the thirteenth and fourteenth centuries. There are said to have been two castles, the 'lower castle', and the 'château du Roi', from which the balliage was administered. The 'lower castle' is said to be connected with a walled town, which is now deserted. The 'château du Roi', of which little survives, is to be found in the present town, whose origins are somewhat later. The 'lower castle' contains four towers. Two were watchtowers, the most interesting and significant towers of this type in Rouergue. They were built on a platform, 80m (262ft) above the river, which can only be reached by ladders. There is a rectangular door at the base of the first tower, and at the top of the tower a small platform looks towards the exterior, to protect the door or to survey the town. To the north, another tower, now truncated, surveyed the valley and town. Only the founda-

Najac. The castle showing the work of Alphonse of Poitiers. (R A Brown)

castle, the 'château du Roi', only a tower remains, but the existing seventeenth century church was derived from one of the castle buildings. The plan of Peyrusse therefore shows the fortification of two successive towns. The ancient town was fortified twice: before 1229, date of the Treaty of Maux, where the Count of Toulouse lost Peyrusse and where the order was given to destroy the walls; and again in the later thirteenth and fourteenth centuries, the period of the surviving walls. The town of the fourteenth to fifteenth centuries, or royal town, was also apparently walled. The evidence for this is in the re-use of the barbican gate.

Bournazel, or what became the barony, is mentioned in a cartulary of Conques in the tenth century. The medieval castle is masked by the construction of a fine Renaissance chateau of the sixteenth century. Nevertheless, two round towers survive, as symbols of a double lordship. They are thought to date from the middle or end of the fifteenth century. One is reminded of earlier, English, examples like Lewes and Lincoln, or French ones like Niort and Touffou.

FORTIFIED TOWNS

The other class of fortification in which the region is very rich, is in new or planted towns – 'bastides' – and in walled villages. The classic bastide has two good examples in Villefranche-de-Rouergue and Villeneuve d'Aveyron. A more irregular and organic town plan survives at Cordes. Of fortified smaller towns or villages, examples were seen at Conques, Varen, and Clairvaux.

Villefranche, upstream from Najac on the Aveyron, was a royal bastide founded in 1252, though the walls were not built until 1342. This is in fact not unusual in bastides, and suggests that their primary role was the extension of influence and jurisdiction, and the encouragement of trade, rather than a predominantly military purpose. Villefranche has a rather curious plan. The north-east and south-east sides suggest a putative rectangle, but the north-west and south-west sides are rounded. The street-plan forms a more or less rectangular grid, but set diagonally to the enceinte. Like most bastides it had a central *place* which contained the market. This occupied two '*insulae*' in the grid, and was entered at all four corners by the main streets, which ran under arcaded *cornières*. In one corner of the *place* is the church. The limits of the town were protected by the Aveyron on one side, and elsewhere by streams which could be used

tions survive of a third tower, discovered in 1959. To the west, a fourth tower was incorporated into the construction of a thirteenth century synagogue. A mural stair gives access to the upper stages. The barbican gate protected the medieval town, and its thirteenth century church of Notre-Dame-de-Laval, which incorporated earlier features, but was abandoned in the sixteenth century. A much restored tower served as a detached belfry, as well as for defence. Up to the fourteenth century, the barbican gate was open to the gorge on the inner, or north, side. However from the end of the fourteenth century, Peyrusse developed towards the south. This new town was walled, and the direction of the barbican gate was reversed by constructing a new door parallel to the first. It may be queried whether any of these monuments should properly be called a 'castle', rather than an elaborate series of town defences, incorporating watchtowers. Of the second

Bruniquel. Twelfth century donjon. *(Author)*

to flood the town ditches. The western part of the walls have emplacements for artillery. It is thought that the peculiarities of the plan were a response to the nature of the terrain, for a hill overlooks the western section of the defences, and obstructs a quadrangular layout here. On the other hand, there may have been a modification of an original plan or concept, and on the face of it this seems more likely.

Villeneuve d'Aveyron has an origin going back to 1053, to the foundation of a monastery of St-Sepulcre-de-Christ. In the twelfth century the Count of Toulouse, like other dominant lords, faced the intrusion into this region of the bishops of Rodez, profiting from the Albigensian crusade. The town was fortified from 1208, but gradually declined after the foundation of Villefranche in 1252. In 1562 it was burnt by the Protestants. The plan of the church was inspired by the Holy Sepulchre at Jerusalem, and originally was circular with apses added at the cardinal points. The town plan appears disorganised, but there is nevertheless an axial east-west road, and six parallel roads which run at right angles to it. A pentagonal market place has *cornières* surviving along two sides. Of the six original gates, only two survive, the Porte Haute, rebuilt in the fourteenth century, and the fifteenth century Porte de Cardaillac, piercing the south wall.

Cordes is a fortified town of a quite diffe-

Peyrusse. The barbican gate. (*J G Coad*)

rent kind. It was founded by Count Raymond VII of Toulouse on a long rocky ridge, which dictated the plan. This eventually consisted of three concentric defences around the bourg, and two more round the faubourgs. It is suggested from the place-name that leather-workers were established at the foot of the hill before 1222. Certainly, in 1273 the town was authorised to hold a fair on the feast of St Bartholomew, patron saint of tanners. In 1226, the Cathars installed weavers at Cordes. The bastide became royal in 1271 after the death of Alphonse of Poitiers, and his wife, daughter of Raymond VII. When peace returned after the defeat of Catharism, the merchants of Cordes became very wealthy, and their opulence is seen in the many fine surviving merchants' houses. The town was pillaged

Cordes. The western gate (Porte des Ormeaux). (A J Taylor)

in the Hundred Years War by brigands and again by the royal troops in 1437. In the sixteenth century the Wars of Religion devastated the region and Cordes, supporting the Catholics, was taken twice by the Protestants. The town never recovered from these two centuries of war, plague, and changing economic circumstances. Even now, it is only summer tourism which keeps it going.

The fortifications of Cordes can be traced in the street plan, in existing lengths of wall, and in the surviving gates. There is a long axial east-west road, and a shorter north-south one, meeting at the market place, near the fortified church. The main gates are at the west and east, complicated by the concentric nature of the defensive circuits. Smaller gates are to north and south. The first, inner, enceinte was restored in the fourteenth century using stones from the earlier walls. The second enceinte is close to the first, and encircles it. Both were constructed between 1222 and 1229. The prosperity of the town rendered the defended area too small, and houses were packed against the walls. The third enceinte provided flanking towers round the outside of the second, and perhaps also had four entrances. The fourth and fifth enceintes protected the suburbs. The fourth encircled the whole town but at some distance out from the earlier walls, while the fifth extended the protection outwards at the east end.

Conques is really little more than a defended village, perched on a small ledge above the Dourdou, a tributary of the Lot. Its chief interest lies in the truly magnificent Romanesque abbey, a pilgrim church with a remarkable *trésor*. The abbey occupies the site of a much earlier monastery. The enceinte of the village defences is sub-rectangular, with four gates in the short sides. There were irregular flanking towers of which one survives. In spite of the difficulties of the terrain, which influenced the plan, the enceinte of the village is in many ways a classic one, ensuring the maximum of defence for the village and monastery within the constraints of resources and geography.

A defended village on an even smaller scale is **Clairvaux**, briefly visited by the conference en route to Conques. The name derives from *de Claris Vallibus*, describing the site of a monastery alleged to have been founded by Alboin, son of Harold Godwinsson of England, and mentioned in a bull of Urban II in 1099. Clairvaux lies, almost isolated, in a sublime valley, and is startling in appearance, being constructed of a deep red sandstone. Like Conques, the defences are approximately rectangular. They incorporate the church, and were probably built in the fourteenth century and repaired in 1412. There are two entrances, a principal gate to the west, formed by a stone tower, and a secondary gate to the north, next to the twelfth century church. There were fine houses in Clairvaux, but no castle is known.

THE CONFERENCE PAPERS

Turning now to the Conference papers one can hint only at their flavour and select a few for comment here. There were wide-ranging regional studies, especially an excellent opening address by the conference organiser, André Debord, which set the scene for the venue and excursions. For Switzerland, Wal-

ter Meyer made an interesting contribution to a little-researched topic, that of unfinished castles. Using archaeological, architectural and documentary evidence, he adduced that in certain places building was begun but never completed. The reasons for failure may have been architectural, topographical, or technical, or connected with political or economic problems.

Tom McNeill had studied early stone castles in Ireland, concluding that these were built by the major lords to reflect their status and resources, at the centres of their lordships, and primarily as products of the establishment and ordering of lordships rather than for the needs of warfare. Earthwork and timber castles were sited more peripherally to lordships, by lesser lords, and

Cordes. Thirteenth century merchant's house, with cornières.
(A J Taylor)

35

had a more purely military function. McNeill thought that the size of the motte, where present, was an indication of the resources and status of the builder. The low numbers of castles in Leinster and Munster could be explained by the tacit acceptance in those areas of the English by the Irish, rendering castles less necessary.

A very stimulating piece of research by J M Poisson was concerned with the Pisan colonisation of Sardinia from the end of the twelfth century, which resulted in a group of castles little known in documents. Many are very imposing and have been the subject of archaeological investigation. Some castles were new; others were existing fortifications, reoccupied. All were for military, judicial or economic control. The new castles of the first half of the thirteenth century are found principally on communication routes, or high points on the coast, in areas of strongest Pisan control, but some were built in unpopulated areas, to attract settlement. It appears that the Pisans introduced into Sardinia a new type of territorial organisation based on a continental model.

Methodological problems were encountered by M Colardelle and E Verdel in their work on lakeside settlements in Isère, particularly at Charavines. This was a high-quality and important excavation of a waterlogged site which produced enigmatic timber buildings and an abundance of environmental evidence. At present it was not possible to be sure of the social status of the inhabitants, or whether indeed the site could be called a castle. Another odd site was in the Gironde, where S Faravel had unexpectedly found a 'maison forte', within a Roman theatre.

Excavation would undoubtedly assist G Pradalie in his investigations of the medieval towers of the Pyrénées Garonnaises. Formerly thought to be signal- or watchtowers, his examination of their character, sites, and environment suggested another interpretation. Their structure is very variable, from very small towers to imposing rectangular buildings, and they also occupy unelevated valley sites, near settlements. Almost all are associated with traces of fortification and habitable terraces. They may in fact be part of castle enceintes, but whether they represent permanent habitations, or occasional refuges for otherwise undefended valley settlements, is not yet known.

In a paper of intense interest to urban specialists, J de Meulemeester described the topographical evidence to be found in a late sixteenth century atlas prepared by Jacques de Deventer for Philip II of Spain, or his father, Charles V. The maps are remarkable in quality and valuable for the study of towns, especially when used in conjunction with archaeological excavations. It is possible to identify the sites of urban fortifications, including castles which might have since disappeared. A dozen coastal towns of the ancient county of Flanders have been examined in this way, showing topographical relationships between the town and the castle. There is further work to be done in the towns of mid-sixteenth century Flanders and Artois.

G Louise had examined the fortifications of the lords of Bellême in the Sâosnais, to the north-west of Maine. At the end of the eleventh century, there was a complex of earthworks, including fifteen castles, and a 16km (10 mile) long linear defence, at the southern frontier of their seigneurie. The system was designed to ensure their strategic and military mastery over their boundaries, to consolidate their hold on the old and new territories of the Sâosnais, and to command the access routes to their capital of Le Mans.

J G Coad in a valuable contribution, showed how some medieval and Tudor fortresses along the southern and south-eastern English coasts threatened by invasion were adapted to meet the needs of later warfare in the 200 years from 1740. Most resources were applied to Dover, where the great medieval castle was extensively modernised and altered between 1740 and 1870, being integrated into a wider coastal defensive system, which included the adaptation in the Napoleonic War period of sixteenth century fortresses.

For Wales, C Caple described recent excavation at the thirteenth and fourteenth century castle of Dryslwyn. Here, as at Charavines, there were waterlogged deposits with evidence of the diet of the occupants. As at other native sites in Wales, a round tower acted as a 'donjon', and other buildings were tailored to the contours.

Of other contributions on single sites, one of the best was by W Ubregts and F Dopere, 'La Fin d'un Donjon Résidential Dans le Nord de la Bélgique', which was a fine example of patient detective work over many years applied to an individual building.

◆

In conclusion, the Fourteenth Château-Gaillard Conference was as interesting and rewarding as its predecessors, and we await the Conference *Proceedings* which are likely to be published in 1989 by the University of Caen, (Centre de Récherches Archéologiques Médiévales).

BERMUDA FORTS – A MILITARY LEGACY

SOME OF THE MOST ELABORATE NINETEENTH CENTURY BRITISH COLONIAL DEFENCES ARE TO BE FOUND IN BERMUDA. DR EDWARD HARRIS OUTLINES THEIR HISTORY AND ARGUES FOR GREATER PUBLIC AWARENESS OF THEIR VALUE

The Bermudas are one of the most isolated island groups in the world. Found at a latitude of 32° North, they are a little over 600 miles (1000km) from the American coast and 3000 miles (4800km) from Britain. The islands of the West Indies lie 1000 miles (1600km) to the south, with Halifax a similar distance northwards.

The islands were settled in 1612 by a group of colonists organized by the Virginia Company, a subsidiary of which, the Bermuda Company, came into being two years later to oversee the exercise. Under the first Governor, Richard Moore, the settlers were obliged to erect some military defences against the Spaniards and other threats. From the Spanish viewpoint, the occupation of Bermuda by the British represented a considerable threat to their treasure fleets homeward bound from Central America and the West Indies. In the days before longitude could be easily established on a ship, Bermuda also served as the northern beacon, the sighting of which gave the pilot his position and immediate bearing for Europe. Many Spanish ships ended up on the Bermuda reefs in their search for this turning point, and the settlement of the islands enhanced its natural dangers with that of a formidable enemy of the Spanish realm.

THE EARLIEST FORTIFICATIONS

Geographically, the eastern end of Bermuda, where settlement and the first town (St George's) were established, was the most vulnerable to attack from the sea. It is there that the reef is broken by several good channels, and extends but a half a mile (800m) from

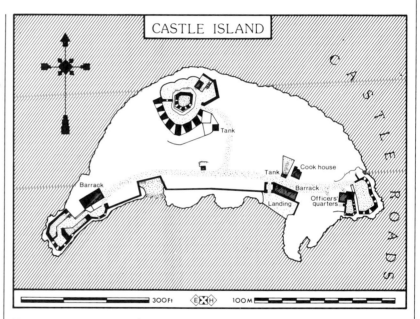

The forts on Castle Island after a survey of 1811; King's Castle faces Castle Roads and Devonshire Redoubt is in the centre. *(All illustrations in this article, by courtesy of the author)*

the land. To the north and west, the platform of reef, often less than 30 feet (9m) deep, reaches out some 5–10 miles (8–16km). Dictated by this topography, the first forts at Bermuda were built on the islands on the eastern coast, adjacent to the two harbours of Castle and St George's. Between 1612 and 1622, about a dozen forts were erected. A depiction of these structures was published by Captain John Smith in his history of Virginia and the Somers Island, as Bermuda was then described in honour of Sir George Somers, wrecked there in 1609 on his way to relieve the starving settlement at Jamestown, Virginia.

These first forts were both lookout towers and coastal redoubts. Of the original number, four survive as considerably intact monuments – recognizable in the descriptions of John Smith, and 50 years older than any sur-

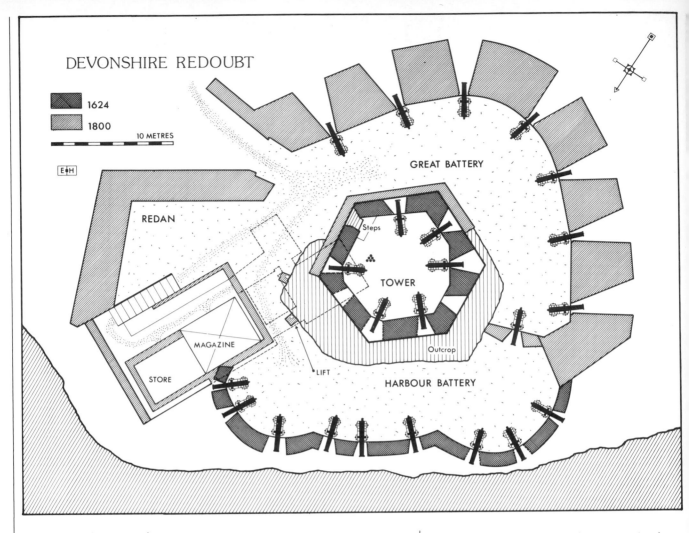

DEVONSHIRE REDOUBT

■ 1624
▨ 1800

10 METRES

GREAT BATTERY

REDAN

Steps

TOWER

MAGAZINE

Outcrop

STORE

LIFT

HARBOUR BATTERY

A survey of Devonshire Redoubt in 1984. The tower and harbour battery date to 1612, the other features to the 1790s.

viving stone fortifications in the continental United States of America. Several more of these early forts survive as archaeological sites awaiting investigation. Three of the forts are located in a nature sanctuary, Castle Island, which has afforded them some protection from people, but little from the encroaching jungle. Two of the forts are noted in Smith's account as the 'King's Castle' and 'Devonshire Redoubt'. A survey of these sites was carried out in 1984 with a team from Brown University under the author's supervision, as there were no known plans of the forts.

It was from the King's Castle in 1613 that the only hostile engagement in the history of Bermuda's forts took place. A Spanish ship had approached the entrance to Castle Harbour which the King's Castle protected and the men armed the fort. A shot was got off at the Spaniards, who turned tail, reporting home in due course about the heavily defended nature of the Bermudas. As Captain Smith reports the truth, the King's Castle had but two cannon balls, and in the process of firing the first, the gunners managed to spill the remainder of the only keg of powder

around the gun, but somehow contrived not to be blown into the sea themselves. So in hilarity did Bermuda's military history begin.

The comedy abated, but fort-building continued apace in the seventeenth century, as can be seen from the plan of the sites of that period. Most of the forts were small coastal batteries for upwards of five guns. They spread along the south and west coast from St George's, the north side of Bermuda containing but one or two batteries. A good number of these batteries built between 1625 and 1783 survive in some form, although most are archaeological remains below ground. The scope for research and archaeological investigation on this group is very large indeed and it is hoped that a programme of work in this vein can be started in the very near future.

THE DOCKYARD AND ITS DEFENCES

By the end of the American Revolutionary War in 1783, Britain had lost all of its mainland ports and naval bases between Canada and the British West Indies. With a constant

Above:
An aerial view of Castle Island from the south-east in 1985.

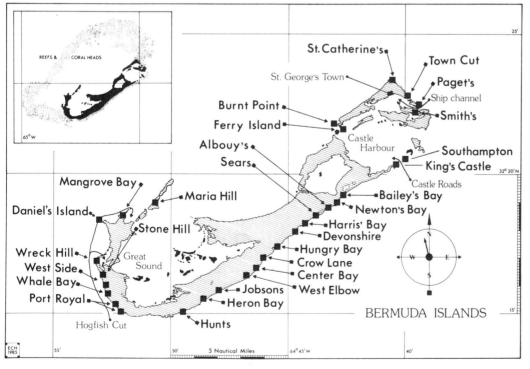

REEFS & CORAL HEADS

65°W

St. Catherine's

Town Cut

St. George's Town

Paget's

Ship channel

Burnt Point

Smith's

Ferry Island

Castle Harbour

Albouy's

Southampton

Sears

King's Castle

25'

32°20'N

Castle Roads

Mangrove Bay

Maria Hill

Bailey's Bay

Daniel's Island

Newton's Bay

Stone Hill

Harris' Bay

Wreck Hill

Devonshire

Great Sound

West Side

Hungry Bay

Whale Bay

Crow Lane

Port Royal

Center Bay

Jobsons

West Elbow

Heron Bay

Hogfish Cut

Hunts

15'

BERMUDA ISLANDS

ECH 1985

55'

50'

5 Nautical Miles

64°45'W

40'

This plan shows the majority of forts at Bermuda around 1700.

threat from the French, and the development of a navy for the new United States of America, the British military strategists lighted on Bermuda as a location for a new naval base and fortified station in the Western Atlantic. Thus, while Bermuda does not contain any great works of the eighteenth century, such as Brimstone Hill in St Kitts in the West Indies, it does have the lion's share of nineteenth century British works on the islands of this hemisphere. And it may be argued that the present rich economic state of the Bermudas is

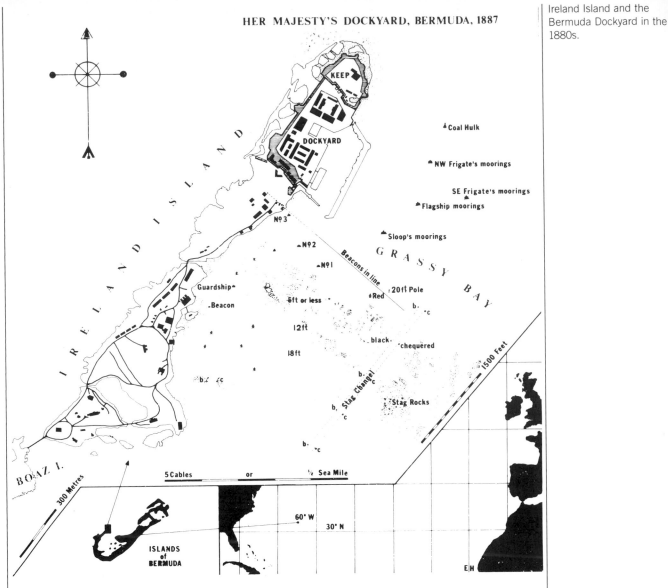

HER MAJESTY'S DOCKYARD, BERMUDA, 1887

Ireland Island and the Bermuda Dockyard in the 1880s.

due to the infusion of the local economy with military money throughout the nineteenth century and early twentieth century. This monetary legacy of the British military was further enhanced by the presence of United States forces during and since the Second World War.

The first flush of British military effort on the Bermuda forts began with the sending of Captain Andrew Durnford, Royal Engineers, to the islands in 1788. After much energetic work, Durnford died at Bermuda a day short of the tenth anniversary of his arrival. He constructed at least four entirely new works to the north of the town of St George's, and made significant repairs and additions to several other forts. An entirely new work, which he called Upper Paget Fort, on Paget Island, was built on the site of the present Fort Cunningham. He employed a number of local slaves and tradesmen on his works, for which many papers are to be found in the holdings of the Bermuda Archives.

To a certain degree, however, Durnford's works fall into the methods of the previous centuries. They were constructed of the soft local stone, as had been the custom for centuries past, and they, as with their predecessors, contained no self-defensive works such as ditches and reverse fires. The great divide in the history of Bermuda fortifications is marked by the work of his successors, when the Royal Engineers began the construction and fortification of the Bermuda Dockyard in the decade following its establishment in 1809 at the western end of the islands, very much to the windward of the town of St George's and the channel entrances. There, at Ireland Island, the Royal Engineers developed a defensive scheme for the 25 acres (10 hectares) of the dockyard. It was to be surrounded on three sides by massive bastioned ramparts, which were begun around 1820, with work accelerated by the importation of convict

40

labour in 1823. This work appears to have been initiated by Captain Thomas Cunningham, RE, but was primarily the brain-child of Major Thomas Blanshard, RE, who spent almost a decade in Bermuda from around 1818. The final arrangement of the land defences and the curtain of the eastern fort, the Keep, was approved in 1827 by the Duke of Wellington, after the receipt of a confidential report by Colonel Edward Fanshawe, RE, who seems to have carried out several secret missions in this part of the Empire.

Thus began the largest construction job in the history of Bermuda, before the Americans built a naval air station near St George's in the early 1940s. Instead of a few martello towers and a defensive ditch, the dockyard was protected on its land front by three outworks, the Couvre-porte, the Ravelin Tower and the Right Advance. Facing these was the rampart of the Land Front, and extending northwards on the west side of the dockyard, was the North-west Rampart flanked by two bastions. Completing the third side of the defences was the Keep, a 6-acre (2.5-hectare) stronghold of seven bastions. Excepting the Ravelin and Couvre-porte, these massive works have survived to the present day.

The Right Advance of the land front of the dockyard defences in 1985.

Fort Victoria in the foreground had two ravelins; the northern one now mounts a 9.2-inch breech loader of 1900. Fort Albert (after its conversion for four 10-inch rifled muzzle loaders) is in the background.

The dockyard defences were finished about 1845, and were rearmed in the 1870s and again in 1900. The dockyard was rebuilt in stone, following a first phase of timbered buildings, and was itself completed about 1860. In support of the defence of the dockyard, it was thought necessary to refortify the eastern approaches to the Narrows Channel (just east of the island of St George's), which had been discovered in Royal Navy hydrographic surveys in the 1790s. This channel lead to the spacious Murray's Anchorage, north of St George's, and westwards to Grassy Bay off the dockyard. Being the only ship channel of significance through the Bermuda reefs, its defence by land batteries was paramount for the preservation of the dockyard and the maintenance of a strong fleet in the Western Atlantic.

St George's Island was most affected by the new fortifications. St Catherine's Fort was completely rebuilt. Swept away in this process were the remains of a battery of 1612, and a position consisting of two redoubts erected by Andrew Durnford in the 1790s. In their place arose a great masonry bastioned work of a similar style to the dockyard defences. Situated on a headland, its land front was defended by a ditch and its entrance by a drawbridge. The ditch was flanked by gunports for carronades in the Keep, located in its centre and highest point within the fort. A subsidiary ditch separating the Keep from the rest of the fort was defended by flanking galleries entered from the Keep.

Further south along the coast, and towards the entrance of the Narrows was a new polygonal redoubt, completed and named after Prince Albert in the early 1840s. Inland and above Fort Albert was Fort Victoria, considered to be the citadel of the defences of St George's Island. This magnificent fort, also of polygonal design, had a central barracks enclosed by a ditch below the *terre-plein* for the guns and the whole fort was protected by a

second ditch – both defended by reverse fires. The fort was much mutilated in the 1960s for a hotel, swimming pool and nightclub.

Lending further landward support on St George's Island were two almost identical redoubts: square works with an internal keep and ditch and an external *terre-plein* for 4 guns. Of these redoubts, Fort William (Western Redoubt) was finished around 1857 but later converted into a glorified powder magazine by roofing over the ditch and keep. Fort George, labelled by Durnford in honour of the third king of that name, was the site of several batteries dating from the origins of the colony. These were replaced by the present Fort George in the 1840s, which was additionally supported on its land front by a martello tower on the south-western end of the island, built in the 1820s by Major Blanshard, and the only such tower of a number planned but never erected.

Lying south-east of St George's and at the mouth of the Narrows is Paget Island, a 20-acre (8-hectare) site which held two of the very first forts built at Bermuda. Paget's Fort flanked the north side of the channel into St George's Harbour, and was complemented to the south by Smith's Fort on Governor's Island. These two sites are today substantial archaeological monuments. Above Paget's Fort in the 1790s, Durnford built a redoubt called Upper Paget Fort, which was demolished in the early 1820s for a new work to defend the entrance to the Narrows.

Fort Cunningham was designed on a polygonal trace and was probably the first fort in Bermuda to be so built. It had a good, deep ditch defended by flanking galleries for musketry fire. It was finished in the early 1820s, or twenty years before the dockyard defences, which were designed with a bastioned trace, a system deemed obsolete by the 1830s. Until the rearmament of the 1870s, Fort Cunningham (named after Thomas Cunningham, RE, its designer) was supplied with ten 24-pounders. None of the other older forts, such as the King's Castle, were altered at this period.

The Bermuda Dockyard from the north-east showing the seven bastions of the Keep, now the Bermuda Maritime Museum.

Fort St Catherine is a work of the 1820s, altered for RMLs in the 1870s. This view is looking south-west.

By 1845, the defences of the new Bermuda Dockyard were complete. Working from the windward side of Bermuda, it was defended by several miles of the western reef. The dockyard was surrounded by works mounting 120 guns, except facing Grassy Bay to the east. Marking out the leeward side, and fronting the Narrows Channel, were Forts Catherine, Victoria, Albert and Cunningham. Protecting their rear were Forts William and George and the martello tower.

NEW TECHNOLOGY AND REARMAMENT 1870–1965

It was on these impressive works that the United States Army sent several officers to spy in the late 1840s. Throughout the nineteenth century, the military threat to the Bermudas was from America and the United States saw the fortified islands as a threat to its authority. According to one British report, the Americans were a nation 'hitherto unable, if not unwilling, to control among its people a wild spirit of aggression dangerous to the maintenance of peace'. Invasion plans were formulated, but never acted upon. The real threat to the Bermuda fortifications of the 1840s, however, came rather from the changing technology of rifled guns and armoured steam-powered ships. So it was that in the 1870s that much of the arduous work of the 1815–45 period was demolished to make way for new weapons and forts.

At the dockyard, the smooth-bore cannon were replaced with rifled muzzle loading guns. On St George's Island, RMLs were added to Forts St Catherine, Albert, Victoria

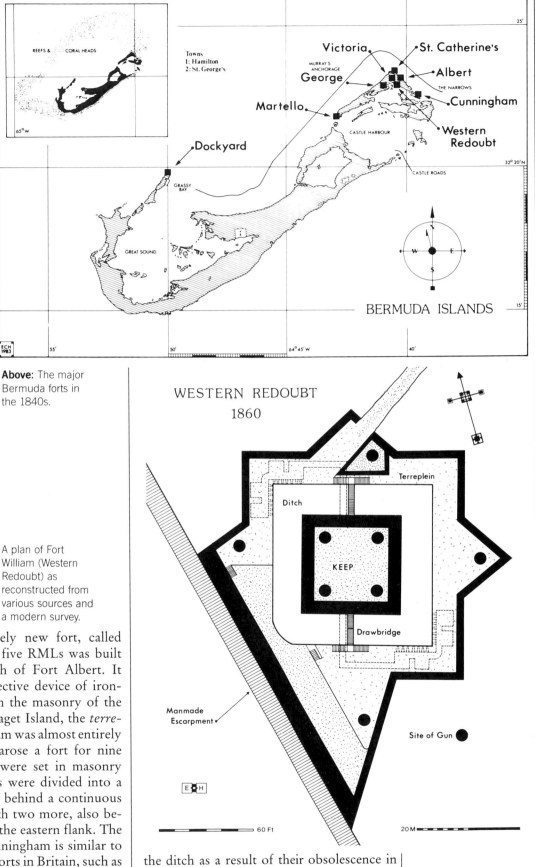

Above: The major Bermuda forts in the 1840s.

WESTERN REDOUBT
1860

A plan of Fort William (Western Redoubt) as reconstructed from various sources and a modern survey.

and George. An entirely new fort, called Alexandra Battery, for five RMLs was built on the coast just south of Fort Albert. It included the new protective device of iron-fronted gunports, set in the masonry of the walls of the fort. On Paget Island, the *terreplein* of Fort Cunningham was almost entirely removed. In its place arose a fort for nine RMLs, two of which were set in masonry embrasures. The others were divided into a main front of five guns behind a continuous straight iron shield, with two more, also behind an iron shield, on the eastern flank. The iron facing at Fort Cunningham is similar to that adopted at several forts in Britain, such as the Plymouth Breakwater Fort, although it differs in having straight fronts, the other forts being circular. The nine RMLs are missing and presumed to be in the seaward run of the ditch as a result of their obsolescence in 1900.

For the first time since colonization, the central parishes of Bermuda now felt the weight of military building. Near the present

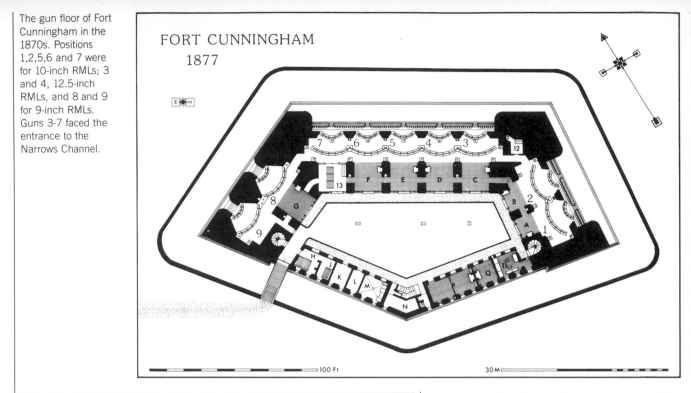

The gun floor of Fort Cunningham in the 1870s. Positions 1,2,5,6 and 7 were for 10-inch RMLs; 3 and 4, 12.5-inch RMLs, and 8 and 9 for 9-inch RMLs. Guns 3-7 faced the entrance to the Narrows Channel.

FORT CUNNINGHAM
1877

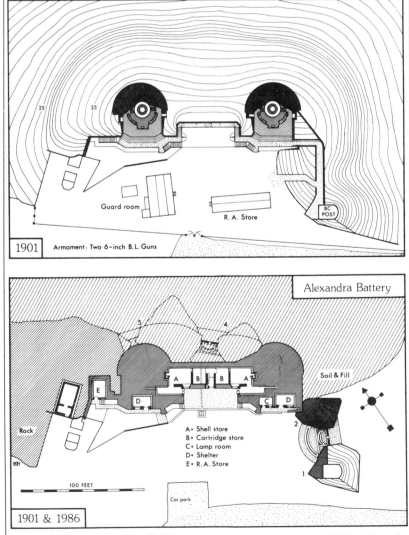

1901   Armament: Two 6-inch B.L. Guns

Alexandra Battery

1901 & 1986

Alexandra Battery gun level, 1901 (upper drawing) and magazines of 1901, with earlier iron fronted gunport of 1875, excavated in 1986, on the lower right.

A • Shell store
B • Cartridge store
C • Lamp room
D • Shelter
E • R. A. Store

capital of Hamilton, the Prospect Position was constructed in the 1870s. It was composed of a south-west to north-east line of three forts: Hamilton, Prospect and Langton. With the exception of three RMLs facing the north shore at Fort Langton, the armament at these forts consisted of 64-pounder RMLs on Moncrieff Disappearing Carriages. Fort Langton was unfortunately demolished in 1984. The purpose of the group was to defend the dockyard against a shelling from the central parishes, should the enemy effect a landing on the beaches of the south shore, where the reef extends but a short distance from the land.

Two other works in this vein were erected in the western parishes. Whale Bay Fort, for three 9-inch RMLs, guarded a small channel to the rear of the dockyard. Scaur Hill Fort (two 64-pounder RMLs) straddled the island of Somerset to prevent a landward attack on the dockyard. In 1985, Collin ('Guns', according to Bermudians) Carpenter identified at Scaur Hill Fort the only known remains of a Moncrieff Disappearing Carriage for this calibre of gun. We have since added two counterweights and a gun (converted Palliser) to this unique collection, which we found elsewhere in Bermuda.

Developments in weapon technology again ruled the day in the last decade of the century, when the fortifications at Bermuda were rearmed with breech loading rifles. Starting in the west, there were four 6-inch BL long range guns at Dockyard, along with three

4.7-inch quick-firing guns and two 12-pounder QF guns for use against torpedo boats. Whale Bay Fort was converted for three 4.7s, and a new battery of two 6-inch BL rifles was built at Warwick Camp in a central position on the south shore of the main island. On St David's Island is found today, according to Victor Smith of the Fortress Study Group, the finest surviving example of a double battery of two 9.2-inch BLs and two 6-inch BLs, erected in the late 1890s. At Fort Cunningham, the RML positions were superseded by new concrete emplacements and two 6-inch BLs. And on St George's Island, Alexandra Battery housed the easternmost guns of this rearmament, which were two 6-inch BLs. This was supported by an emplacement for two 9.2s on the north side of Fort Victoria.

After the First World War, many of these guns were dismounted. Warwick Camp and St David's Battery were brought back into service with re-tubed barrels for the 6-inch guns in time for the 1939–45 conflict, the latter position serving as an Examination Battery for suspect shipping. Evidence also remains of American gun emplacements of that period.

FUTURE PROSPECTS

That is of the past: what of today and this splendid military legacy? First, the forts of Bermuda have little protection under the law. A bill passed in 1913 to protect the early forts of Castle Island is but paper in legal archives. The majority of these sites passed into the hands of the Bermuda Government in the early 1950s, at a time when there was little appreciation of their historic and economic value (to tourism), and at a time when – believe it or not – Bermuda was a very poor place indeed. Archaeological sites on land in Bermuda have no protection whatever.

Of the fifty or so known sites of forts, only six are under any form of guardianship. The others languish on government lands, a neg-

Whale Bay Fort mounted three 4.7-inch quick-firing guns in its final phase in 1900-20.

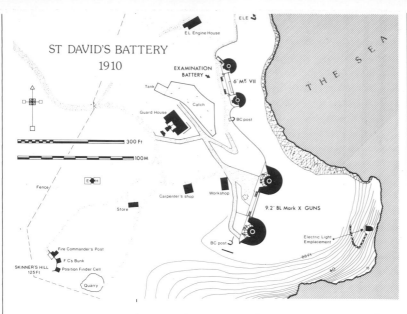

ST DAVID'S BATTERY
1910

300 Ft
100 M

Fence

E●H

Store

Carpenter's shop   Workshop

SKINNER'S HILL
125 Ft

Fire Commander's Post

F C's Bunk

Position Finder Cell

Quarry

EL Engine House

EXAMINATION
BATTERY

Tank

Guard House

Catch

BC post

6" M⨍ VII

9.2" BL Mark X GUNS

BC post

Electric Light
Emplacement

T H E S E A

65 Ft

the trail, several years ago.

Most of Bermuda's forts survive as standing monuments or archaeological remains. The time is ripe to secure them for the future, if government officials can be persuaded of their intrinsic worth and value to the tourist trade. The Bermuda Maritime Museum leads the field in research and by practical example of what can be done. In an important recent move, the Bermuda National Trust has established committees on land archaeology and military sites, which augurs well for the future prospects of the forts. International opinion, however, is a vital influence towards this preservation movement. It is to be hoped that this new magazine, *Fortress*, will attract those who can assist Bermudians and others in the saving and enhancing of their military legacies of forts, guns, and other monuments to man's perennial inability to live in harmony with others.

Further Reading

The author has published several articles on Bermuda forts in recent issues of *Post-Medieval Archaeology*. For a general guide to these monuments, a 40-page booklet, *Great Guns of Bermuda*, and a study of the nineteenth century works, *Bulwark of Empire*, are available from the Bermuda Maritime Museum (for this latter see the Book Reviews section).

Above: St David's Battery still mounts its four 6-inch and 9.2-inch breech loading rifles and is now part of a national park.
Below: Scaur Hill Fort had two 64-pounder RMLs on Moncrieff disappearing carriages. One gun was in the fort, the other in a detached emplacement to the left.

lected, but potentially enormous, asset. These forts range in date from 1612 to 1945 and, remarkably, contain into the bargain, a considerable range of historic ordnance. The Bermuda Maritime Museum (which is restoring the dockyard Keep), for example, has recently restored the only known example of a 40-pounder Armstrong breech loader (dated 1864) on a siege carriage. It was found in a private garden, missing its wheels and part of

The publishers of *Fortress* announce the launch of a specialist imprint dedicated to top quality reference books in the same fields of interest as the journal itself. The emphasis will be on new titles, but some of the classic works will be made available once more in reprinted editions. The first two titles are described below.

FORTRESS BRITAIN
Artillery Fortification in the British Isles and Ireland

by Andrew Saunders

Although many books have been written about the medieval castle and its development, this is the first complete survey of British artillery fortifications since the late Middle Ages, utilizing modern historical and archaelogical findings.

While it is comphrehensive and fully documented, *Fortress Britain* is also highly readable and illustrated throughout with a superb collection of photo-

graphs, contemporary plans and diagrams. Finally, its value as a work of reference is enhanced by an extensive Gazetteer, giving details of every site accessible to the public in Britain and Ireland.

270 × 200mm, 256 pages, 190 photographs, 65 plans, maps and line drawings. ISBN 1 85512 000 3.
£20.00
Publication 26 June 1989

FORTIFICATION:
Its Past Achievements, Recent Developments, and Future Progress

by Sir George Sydenham Clarke

One of the most controversial books on the subject in its day, and one of the most influential, *Fortification* was originally written to remove the subject of fixed defences from the rarified atmosphere of the military specialists and open it up for public debate. Therefore its historical survey was lucid, free from jargon and totally accessible to the layman, despite providing a thoughtful analysis of the development of siege warfare.

Although it went through many editions in its day, *Fortification* is now a very rare book indeed. However, apart from its value to collectors and specialists, it is still one of the best general accounts of fortress warfare since the Renaissance. This new impression is reprinted from the expanded second edition of 1907 and is complete with all the original fine-line engravings.

225 × 152mm, 384 pages, 32 plates, 27 diagrams.
ISBN 1 85512 005 4. **£25.00**
Publication 26 June 1989

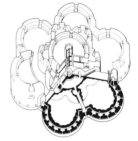

TIMBER CASTLES – A REASSESSMENT

THE USE OF TIMBER IN MEDIEVAL FORTIFICATIONS WAS MORE WIDESPREAD AND LASTED LONGER THAN IS GENERALLY BELIEVED. IN A PREVIEW OF HIS FORTHCOMING BOOK, DR ROBERT HIGHAM CONSIDERS THE EVIDENCE, AND CONCLUDES THAT THE CASTLE OF THE EARLY MIDDLE AGES LOOKED VERY DIFFERENT FROM ITS POPULAR IMAGE

The medieval castle – the popular image (Caernarvon). *(Author)*

The vast majority of us will at some stage in our lives have heard of, read of, seen in book, magazine or on television something referred to as a 'castle'. A smaller, but still very large number of us will have seen such a place for ourselves, either in passing or on a visit. It is probably castles, together with great churches and monasteries, which most readily evoke an image of the Middle Ages in popular imagination. This in itself is not unreasonable, since these were certainly very impressive parts of the medieval landscape in both their size and their building technology. But how true a reflection of that landscape are the castles which attract large numbers of visitors, which are illustrated in most publications as well as on postcards, calendars, tea-towels and the rest? These castles impinge upon our view of the past, as well as upon our view of our contemporary surroundings, for one simple reason: they were built of stone, whose durable quality provides something to look at centuries later, even if extensively ruined.

Yet those who have studied medieval castles in greater depth will know that such castles were not the only ones to have existed. Our landscape also contains large numbers of castle sites represented only by earthworks on which there are no buildings surviving above ground at all. They take many forms, a com-

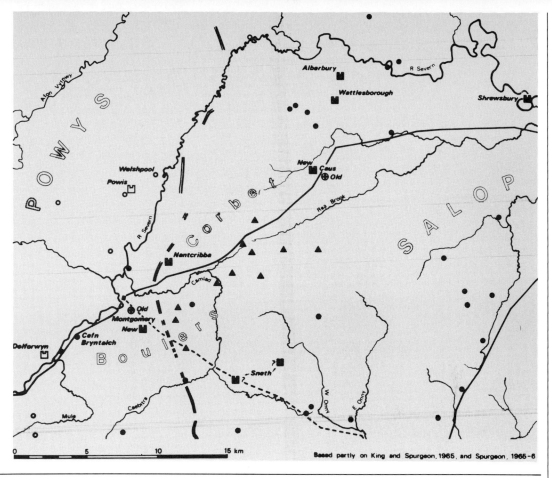

Based partly on King and Spurgeon, 1965, and Spurgeon, 1965–6

■ NORMAN STONE CASTLE
Ⓜ WELSH STONE CASTLE
▲ VALE OF MONTGOMERY
  MOTTE (NORMAN)
● NORMAN EARTHWORK CASTLE
○ WELSH EARTHWORK CASTLE
▟ OFFA'S DYKE
╱ ROMAN ROAD
⋰ POSSIBLE ROMAN ROAD
▭ LAND OVER 244 m

Medieval castles of the Montgomery Region

This landscape of castles on part of the Welsh border illustrates the problem of studying timber castles historically. Whereas the larger (named) sites, often stone built, have some documented history, many of the earthwork sites have no known history whatever, though some (shown by the symbol ▲) were referred to collectively in 1224-25. (Author)

mon one being the motte and bailey in which a large mound of earth and/or rock dominates a defended courtyard. These earthworks carried the same mixture of defensive and residential structures that are found in stone castles, but with an important difference: they were built of timber, clay-clad timber, cob, wattle and daub, shingles and thatch. The total decay of these materials above ground leaves traces which are recoverable only through meticulous excavation. To uncover this information in a useful quantity takes long and painstaking work. The author has for many years been involved in the excavation of a motte and bailey castle at Hen Domen (Montgomery, Powys).[1] This has revealed a complex sequence of buildings stretching from the late eleventh to the thirteenth centuries. The contrast between the open, attractive character of the earthworks and the crowded and oppressive nature of the site as built and occupied is enormous. The complexity of the site has also another dimension, for while as a monument it is *one* castle, in medieval times it had several social identities which arose from the changing pattern of its ownership and occupation. Initial perusal of the evidence published for other comparable sites confirmed this impression gained

from Hen Domen: timber castles have a far more interesting structural and social history than is generally appreciated. Their importance was clearly stated by those writers who put castle studies on a modern footing at the beginning of the present century. Nevertheless, they receive little more than brief acknowledgement in the majority of books, whose authors have been concerned above all to describe the development of stone castles. To fill this gap in the literature a book devoted to timber castles is currently being prepared.[2] The main themes of this study are outlined here.

THE HISTORICAL EVIDENCE

Since the detailed structural evidence of timber castles can be studied only through excavation, discussion of the subject tends to have an archaeological bias. It is also true that there is an historical dimension to timber castles. There are certainly fewer documentary materials than exist for the study of stone castles. Nevertheless a surprising amount of information can be gleaned from a wide array of sources. Where stone and timber castles differ in this respect, however, is in the coverage of written sources *vis-à-vis* the total archaeological evidence. Whereas the

Now crowned by a nineteenth century rebuild of a fourteenth century shell-keep, the motte at Durham carried an elaborate timber tower in the early twelfth century which was described in detail by Laurence, prior of Durham, *c*1150. *(Author)*

identity of all but a few stone castles is known from documents, there are large numbers of earthworks, sites of former timber castles, which are completely unknown to history. Some were established at an early period, when documentary sources for medieval life in general were less full. Others were built by families whose activities were not recorded by contemporary writers because they had little or no impact on local or national affairs. Others still had a very brief existence, built and occupied in time of war and having little social or institutional life. It follows that the precise dating of many timber castle sites poses severe difficulty.

Allowing for such difficulties, the framework of timber castle dating is nevertheless clear enough. In France they were in use by the tenth century, perhaps earlier, and by the late twelfth century were widespread in most parts of western Europe. It is commonly assumed that timber castles were only significant at an early date. This is quite untrue. There is plenty of documentary evidence to demonstrate their use in the thirteenth and early fourteenth centuries, both in the continuing occupation of old sites and the establishment of new ones. In addition, many timber castles were gradually rebuilt in stone, having a mixed character for part of their lives. Even in so-called 'stone castles' there was

much more timber than often supposed. Not only was timber an ingredient of all stone buildings, in floors, roofs *et cetera*, it was also used for complete residential buildings as well as for defensive structures. Large numbers of stone castles had outer defences of timber in the thirteenth and fourteenth centuries and timber galleries projecting from their stone wall-tops. Even some major timber structures survived to this date: the timber motte tower at Shrewsbury eventually collapsed *c*1270.

Some documentary references to timber castles also reveal something about their structural character, though large numbers do not. Many of the well-known components of stone castles had their timber counterparts. We hear of palisades, of gateways, of bridges, of perimeter towers and of domestic buildings. But what struck contemporaries most were the great towers, which in stone castles we would call 'keeps', which rose from their mottes and provided both the main residence and the ultimate defence of the castle. Some of these, as described by contemporary chroniclers, were complex and ornate buildings. In England, for example, the episcopal castle at Durham had a magnificent motte-tower of timber in the early twelfth century. Such descriptions are, however, few in number, and for a more detailed structural view of timber castles other sources must be used.

THE PROBLEMS OF PICTORIAL EVIDENCE

Closest in character to the documentary sources are sources with pictorial evidence for timber castles. Though few in number they are of great interest. They include the famous embroidery known as the Bayeux Tapestry, stone sculpture, wood-carving, manuscript illustration and painting. Whereas the cumulative evidence of documentary references and of surviving earthworks will allow some generalisation to be made, the pictorial sources are so individualistic that great care must be exercised in their interpretation. The best way to illustrate this briefly is by reference to one particular example.

The Bayeux Tapestry, in its depiction of the Norman conquest of England and the events which led up to it, provides illustrations of various castles in northern France and of Hastings in southern England. The scene illustrating the construction of Hastings is well-known, commonly used as evidence in the debate on both the chronology and physical form of English castle origins. At first sight, this evidence is simple enough: workmen are throwing soil upwards to form a motte on top of which stands a timber palisade. But in fact there are fundamental problems. First, are we viewing the building operations in proper sequence? The fact that the motte surface is already capped with a continuous deposit when the main layers themselves (lying horizontal, an unusual pattern though known from some excavations) are still being thrown up raises doubts here. Perhaps the designer 'telescoped' successive events. Equally, the outer surface may simply be an artistic device with no structural significance at all – a major consideration for the use of any pictorial source. The same problem of 'telescoping' applies to the structure on the motte top. Are we viewing what was eventually put there, or what was already there – was the motte being thrown up around it? Both types of construction are plausible and known from excavated examples. A century later, the Norman poet Wace wrote that Hastings castle had been of prefabricated timber construction, transported with duke William's fleet from Normandy. Though this tradition has sometimes been discredited because of its late date, it deserves more attention. By the twelfth century such practice was quite common, and it could have had earlier

The construction of Hastings castle as depicted on the Bayeux Tapestry. *(By courtesy of Phaidon Press Ltd)*

origins (at Hen Domen excavated evidence has demonstrated some prefabrication in the castle erected in the 1070s). If Hastings was built in this way it would make good practical sense to erect the structure and pile the motte around it. But here another difficulty presents itself, for the Tapestry shows not a tower rising from the motte, which we would expect, but a palisade. Here there is a strong contrast with its depiction of castles in northern France, whose mottes carry tall buildings. The second major problem lies in the date of the Tapestry's production, which was a decade after 1066. Since it was produced in southern England, it should be reliable in its evidence. Yet the designer may have been portraying what he was familiar with in Norman England of the 1070s, rather than what actually took place in 1066 at Hastings. The Tapestry undoubtedly gives us an informative depiction of castle-building, but does it necessarily apply to Hastings in particular? This we can never know. Excavation here produced no structural timber evidence of eleventh century date. Indeed the existing motte at Hastings may not even date from the conquest at all, since part of the site was destroyed by coastal erosion centuries ago.

RELATED TIMBER STRUCTURES

Given the extensive reconstruction in stone of so many timber castles and the organic nature of the building materials concerned it is hardly surprising that no timber castle, or even part of one, survives intact. There are, however, survivals of timber, or partly timber buildings within stone castles. At Leicester, the timber arcades of an aisled hall of very high quality survive in fragmentary form from the mid-twelfth century. At Tamworth (Staffs), an early fifteenth century timber-framed hall stands within the twelfth century shell keep. At Stokesay (Shropshire), the timber storey which projects from the north tower, though now owing much to seventeenth century reconstruction, was contemporary in its original form with the late thirteenth century stonework immediately below. From numerous excavations pieces of waterlogged timber have been recovered. These sometimes show evidence of carpentry techniques. At der Husterknupp (Rhineland) uprights from domestic buildings had been chamfered where they emerged from their post-holes. At Hen Domen the base of a 12ft-wide motte bridge survived *in situ*, and from the bailey ditch came parts of the baseplate of a free standing palisade made of jointed upright planks.

From other types of medieval timber building some of the character of timber castles may be indirectly inferred. The development of framed domestic buildings, which survive in great numbers in town and country from the fourteenth and fifteenth centuries, overlapped with the period when timber castles were still in use. From earlier times, other structures may be helpful, such as the twelfth century timber aisled barn of the Knights Templar at Cressing (Essex). The thirteenth century monastic barn at Great Coxwell (Berks) may also convey something of the right atmosphere, for although its external walls are of stone, the upper parts of its aisle posts and its open roof are of timber. The stave-built timber churches of Norway are another useful parallel. Their high achievement in decorative detail by the thirteenth century is a reminder that timber castles need not always have been plain. Indeed the castles depicted in the Bayeux Tapestry have some decorative carving. Builders of stone castles certainly paid attention to detail, and timber castles owned by kings, bishops and rich nobles need not have been less well treated.

Perhaps the structures which most closely relate to the timber castles we know from documentary and pictorial sources, as well as from excavation, are the belfries (sometimes detached) such as those in Essex, Kent, on the Welsh border and elsewhere. Several have been dated by their carpentry techniques and/or scientific dating to the twelfth or thirteenth centuries in their original form. Brookland (Kent), Navestock (Essex) and Pembridge (Hereford) are well-known examples and there are several more. The cross-braced construction of these belfries is reminiscent of an early twelfth century stone-carving of a castle at Modena, northern Italy. That the surviving examples are belfries is perhaps no coincidence, for the word 'belfry' originally meant a timber tower used in siege warfare. Towers of this type could have a wide application – on or in mottes, on bailey perimeters, and in sieges. Perhaps the *bretasches*, to which reference in the twelfth and thirteenth centuries is common, were not dissimilar. These were often of prefabricated construction, to which towers built in this way would easily lend themselves.

ARCHAEOLOGY AND THE TIMBER CASTLE

The archaeological evidence for timber castles takes broadly two forms. From excavations comes structural evidence in fascinating detail. But for every excavated site there are

Stokesay, Shropshire. The lower part of the north tower is of mid-thirteenth century date. The upper part, built in the 1290s, carried a projecting timber storey some of which survives in the existing fabric. *(Author)*

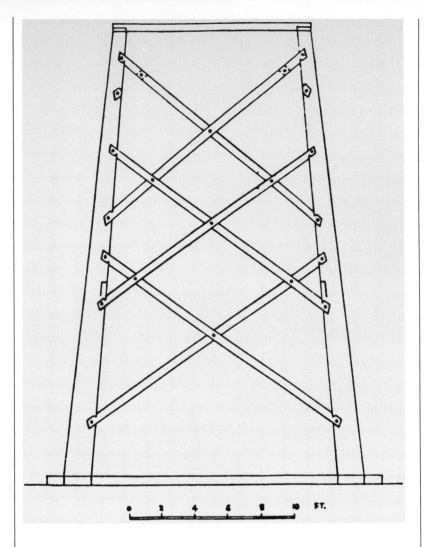

The timber belfry at Brookland, Kent. Standing on a 15-foot square base and framed with diagonal members and notched-lap joints, this timber tower was originally nearly 30 feet high and probably had a projecting roofed platform. *(By courtesy of K Gravett)*

Opposite, top: Though no doubt open to revision in detail, this map shows the wide distribution and clustering of British mottes, which were commonly timber-built in their early phases and sometimes throughout their lives.
(By courtesy of Derek Renn)

countless others whose earthworks remain unexplored. From these, deductions of a more general nature must be made. The most obvious lesson to be learned is the enormous quantity and wide distribution of the evidence in the field. It extends from Ireland in the west, from Scotland and Denmark in the north, eastwards into Germany, and southwards through France into Italy. It is impossible to offer precise numbers of sites. While many of them are the characteristically medieval mottes (with or without baileys), others are enclosures of varying shape and size (sometimes called ringworks) which are not always easily distinguished from sites of earlier date. In any case, estimates of numbers are meaningless historically, since many sites have already been destroyed and since excavation sometimes reveals that earthworks contain stone, not timber structures. It is the overall quantity which matters – and there are several thousand. Also of interest are variations in distribution density: political and cultural frontiers are sometimes thickly studded with these (and other) castles, for example the Welsh Marches or the Rhineland. There is

no doubt whatever that timber castles were an enormously important feature of the medieval landscape. In the eleventh and twelfth centuries they must have outnumbered stone castles by a considerable margin. And although some timber castles fell out of use during the twelfth century, many continued in occupation alongside increasingly important military architecture in stone. It is a weakness of the archaeological study of castles that emphasis falls on improvement, innovation and development. It is easy to forget that for every up-to-date site in the landscape of castles there were many more of a less sophisticated nature, relicts of an earlier style of castle design. And for many of the less rich among the landowning class such sites continued to be of value.

Fieldwork on the earthwork sites of timber castles has a number of applications. First, it is only by detailed survey, on the ground and from air photographs, that the precise character of a site can be demonstrated. Field record sometimes hints at the location of buried features and at the relative chronology of different parts of a site – not all the earthworks may be contemporary. Field survey may also reveal the relationship of a castle site to an adjacent settlement, as is the case at Stafford. In the present century, steadily improving standards of survey, practised notably by the various Royal Commissions on Historical Monuments in Great Britain, have produced a much more reliable body of field evidence than was available to earlier students of castle studies. Comparative use of detailed site surveys, backed up by further personal observation, underlies attempts to make sense of the enormous quantity of field evidence through classification. Mottes have been categorized according to shape and height, and their position *vis-à-vis* their baileys. Enclosure or ringwork sites have been categorized according to their size and the profile of their defences. Such classification certainly demonstrates the character of the evidence and the various ways in which earthwork forms could be employed. But there is a limit to what can be achieved in this way. It does not follow that superficially similar sites are of the same date. Given the long period of time during which timber castles were appearing and disappearing, there is a danger of drawing together in categories sites which may have little to connect them historically. Field survey also illustrates how varied in detail the sites are. Their individuality is further emphasised when the results of excavation are taken into account. A general weakness of study through survey

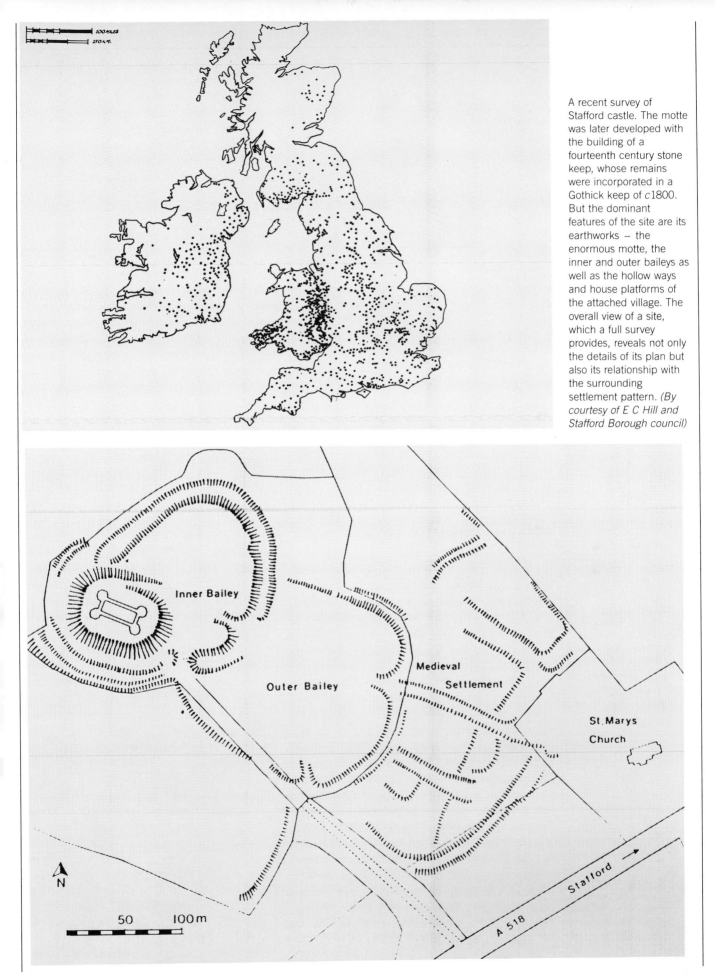

A recent survey of Stafford castle. The motte was later developed with the building of a fourteenth century stone keep, whose remains were incorporated in a Gothick keep of *c*1800. But the dominant features of the site are its earthworks – the enormous motte, the inner and outer baileys as well as the hollow ways and house platforms of the attached village. The overall view of a site, which a full survey provides, reveals not only the details of its plan but also its relationship with the surrounding settlement pattern. *(By courtesy of E C Hill and Stafford Borough council)*

Inner Bailey

Outer Bailey

Medieval Settlement

St. Marys Church

N

50   100m

A 518   Stafford

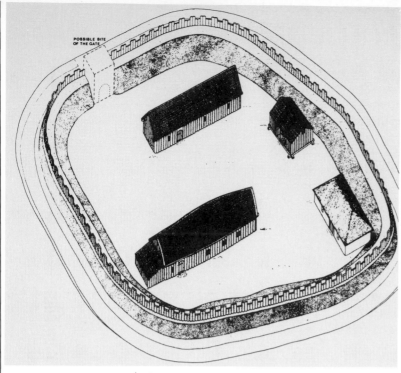

Goltho, Lincolnshire: a reconstruction of the defences and buildings *c*850 AD. Goltho is one of a number of places where excavation has revealed earlier phases of sites where mottes were not primary features. *(By courtesy of G Beresford)*

fore the Normans arrived, there are similar complexities. In the late twelfth century some existing sites were filled in and raised into mottes. This occurred at Castleskreen, Ballynarry and Rathmullan (all in Co Down). Recent excavations have also suggested that some Irish sites were very similar to mottes even before the Norman invasion took place. Information from such sites raises very basic questions about the origins of castles.

From excavation we can also see how sites occupied for long periods were subject to periodic rebuilding and redesign. At Launceston (Cornwall) and Sandal (Yorkshire) timber castles were gradually transformed into stone in the twelfth century. Much evidence about timber castles, extensively disturbed by subsequent activity, must underlie many stone castles. At Hen Domen there was an almost continuous process of repair and rebuilding in the bailey between the late eleventh and the thirteenth centuries, but this was exclusively of timber. The major phases of reconstruction

alone is that the field monuments survive in a form which mainly reflects their final development. Only excavation can reveal the potentially complex sequence of occupation lying beneath, which has sometimes involved drastic alterations to the site.

THE STRUCTURAL DEVELOPMENT OF TIMBER CASTLES

Excavation has, without any doubt, transformed our understanding of timber castles. There was virtually no excavated evidence available to Mrs Ella Armitage and others who put British castle studies on a firm footing at the beginning of this century. Indeed, most of the excavations on timber castle sites have taken place in the last forty years. There have been numerous explorations, though few conducted on a large scale. One of the most striking results is the discovery of whole phases of sites which were otherwise invisible. At der Husterknupp (Rhineland), Mirville (Normandy) and Goltho (Lincs, England), sites which had mottes by the late eleventh century had originally been very different. Starting as defended enclosures they were transformed by successive generations of occupants. Drastic changes have also been observed at other sites. At Neroche (Somerset) a pre-conquest enclosure was redesigned by the Normans and only in the twelfth century was a motte built at one end of the site. In Ireland, where there was a long-established tradition of rath construction be-

were very different in character from each other. A hypothetical visitor to the site would have seen very contrasting views c1080, c1150 and c1230. The earliest castle was simple and massive, its bailey dominated by a great hall in front of the bridge leading to the motte, and a granary some yards away. The twelfth century castle was crowded with buildings of all sorts – the atmosphere within must have been very claustrophobic. The latest castle was far less densely built-up, occupation contracting towards the motte. These contrasts reflect the changing social history of the site. At its foundation it was an instrument of Norman conquest in Wales. At its end it was subordinate to a new castle of stone built a mile (1.6km) away at Montgomery by Henry III. In between it had been the main residence and administrative centre of a small Marcher lordship. Not even the most sophisticated field survey of the site could have even hinted at its complexity.

As well as overall views of structural de-velopment, excavation also reveals individual buildings of great interest. Many excavators have dissected mottes, or at least parts of mottes. Abinger (Surrey) became well-known for its rectangular timber tower and its surrounding palisade built on top of the motte. At South Mimms (Middlesex), a timber tower had a motte thrown up around it, and the motte itself was revetted in timber. At Lismahon (Co Down), a house on dry-stone footings had a slender, timber tower at one end and a surrounding palisade. These varying examples illustrate the individuality of motte structures, which must reflect one aspect of their history. But is it the whole story? Evidence of towers within mottes might only survive at their very bases, so that excavation of only their upper portions might be quite misleading. Timberwork on the outer faces of eroded mottes might be equally elusive. A fully-framed tower standing on a motte might leave virtually no evidence in the ground at all. The use of such structures might explain the

P. Scholefield . 87

The medieval castle – an alternative image. Reconstruction of the northern half of the bailey, c1150, at Hen Domen, Montgomery (Powys). This drawing and the excavated evidence upon which it is based are discussed fully in *Current Archaeology* X, No 4 (September 1988), pp137-142. *(Drawing by P Scholefield)*

apparently empty tops of some excavated mottes. Despite numerous excavations we have hardly begun to understand one of the most common classes of medieval field monument. Only total excavation can reveal the full story of a motte's development, and for various reasons this is normally an impossible task.

The excavation of the baileys which accompanied mottes, and of the interiors of enclosure castles, has produced a similarly varied picture. Ramparts, examined for example at Hen Domen, Therfield (Herts), Lydford (Devon), Launceston (Cornwall) and Ludgershall (Wilts) could be piled around their palisade timbers, revetted at front and/or back, or have their palisades dug into their tops. Domestic buildings occur in all shapes and sizes. In the twelfth century phase at Hen Domen there were two halls, a chapel, a granary, water cistern, a small house and workshop, and other small rooms tucked into the back of the defences. There was also a structural division across the middle of the bailey, creating an extra line of defence and also a social distinction between 'upper' and 'lower' halves. Other sites have also produced domestic ranges, or parts of them, with halls and ancillary buildings, for example Sandal (Yorkshire), Barnard Castle (Co Durham) and Llantrithyd and Rumney (both in Glamorgan). In contrast at Launceston (Cornwall) and Lydford (Devon) the late eleventh century plans contained rows of small buildings, perhaps quarters for an army of conquest rather than high-quality accommodation.

◆

Generally, however, timber castles seem to have contained buildings of similar form and function to those surviving in stone castles. This reminds us that we should not view timber castles as a separate 'type' of castle, but rather as a variation on a theme. Castle designers aimed to meet similar requirements of defence and residence with whatever building technology and materials were at their disposal. Timber might be chosen because no suitable stone was available, or because the builder could not afford to buy stone, or because speed of erection was essential, or because only short-term use for the site was envisaged. The structures referred to briefly above were built in many ways. Some had ground-fast individual posts, others had posts built in trenches, others had walls laid on horizontal base-plates, and others were set on dry-stone footings. Some used much timber, others employed much wattle and daub. Some

made extensive use of clay, so that the timbers were hardly visible. In their use of such practices the designers of castles were part of a very long tradition of European building technique. Timber building stretched back into prehistory and was still flourishing in the seventeenth century (later in some areas). Adapted for the most part to providing domestic accommodation, timber building had also been regularly exploited for defensive needs. Prehistoric hillforts, Roman camps, Celtic strongholds, early town defences – all had employed timber and earthwork technology. And the tradition extended far beyond western Europe into the Slav lands of the east. Timber castles were firmly rooted in the culture of the northern world. Their general reassessment is long overdue.

Notes

[1] P A BARKER, R A HIGHAM, *Hen Domen, Montgomery: a timber castle on the English-Welsh border* (Roy Arch Inst monograph series, 1982)

[2] P A BARKER, R A HIGHAM, *Timber Castles* (Batsford, London; forthcoming)

Acknowledgement

I am indebted to my colleague Philip Barker for our continuing discussion of this topic, and to many others for advice which will be acknowledged in the volume referred to.

Notes on contributors

Dr Edward Harris, Director of The Bermuda Maritime Museum, has written numerous articles on aspects of the defences of Bermuda. He has also published his important excavations at Sandgate Castle, Kent, and is author of *Principles of Archaeological Stratigraphy.*

Dr Robert Higham is a lecturer in the Department of History and Archaeology at the University of Exeter. He is secretary of the recently founded Castles Studies Group, and is an authority on south-western castles as well as co-director of the excavations at the castle of Hen Domen near Montgomery.

Dr Stephen Johnson is a Principal Inspector of Ancient Monuments with English Heritage and is editor of its Academic and Specialist Publications. Author of *Late Roman Fortifications* and *The Roman Forts of the Saxon Shore*, his new book on Hadrian's Wall appears in the spring of 1989.

Christine Mahany is a medieval archaeologist who has worked chiefly in Lincolnshire. One of her major excavations was on the site of Stamford Castle. She is currently an archaeological consultant working for English Heritage.

Dr Denys Pringle is a Principal Inspector of Ancient Monuments with Historic Scotland, Scottish Development Department. A former student at the British School of Archaeology in Jerusalem he is an authority on castles in the Near East. He has recently edited a new edition of, and contributed an introduction to, T E Lawrence's *Crusader Castles.*

THE ARMADA:
1588–1988

As we are all well aware, 1988 was 'Armada Year'. There were celebrations at Plymouth, the lighting of beacons, pageants of one sort or another across the country, and analysis on television. There was a prestigious exhibition at the National Maritime Museum, Greenwich, and later at Belfast, to which Spanish and other museums and archives generously contributed. These events were a celebration of the deliverance from invasion and victory at sea four hundred years ago. In particular, they emphasised the sighting and pursuit of the Great Armada up the Channel, the action off Gravelines, and the disastrous dispersal of the fleet by hard weather round the coasts of the England, Scotland and Ireland. The celebrations focussed, understandably, on aspects maritime. Little attention was given to contemporary activities on land and the measures taken to repel the anticipated invasion when it came, whether from the forces on board the Armada or from those of the Duke of Parma transported from the Spanish Netherlands as well.

It is understandable that the defences on land get little mention. There was no invasion, few impressive new permanent fortifications had been initiated by the Elizabethan government, and the widespread defence works which were constructed were of a temporary nature and are scarcely visible today. At the start of her reign, Queen Elizabeth had inherited the expensive scheme for creating a border fortress at Berwick-upon-Tweed, and, in the first year of her reign, a small fort was built at Upnor on the north bank of the Medway to protect the new naval anchorage at Chatham. No other major piece of fortification was undertaken until 1584 when relations between England and Spain were deteriorating fast. This involved the re-fortification of the town and dockyard of Portsmouth,

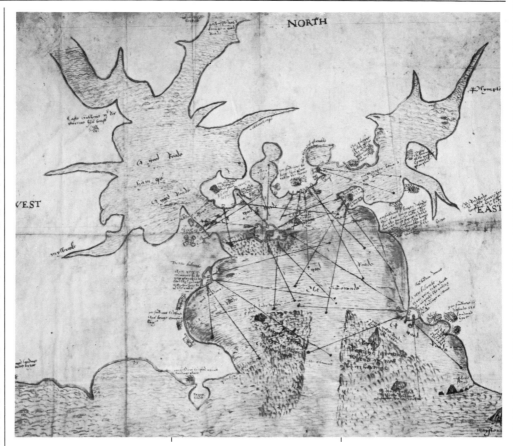

Contemporary map of Plymouth used by Mark Brayshay in the article mentioned below. *(PRO)*

and together with some improvements to the medieval enceinte of Carisbrooke Castle, Isle of Wight, was all that was done in the way of new permanent defence works. Otherwise there were the obsolete castles and blockhouses, mainly erected by Henry VIII, along the southern and eastern coasts to meet another invasion crisis nearly 50 years earlier.

To suppose that these limited established fortifications were the sum of invasion preparations in anticipation of the Armada is to ignore those other elements of defence: the early warning systems of patrolling ships and an elaborate beacon system, the development and training of the militia into a numerous, if unreliable, 'Home Guard', and the profusion of earthworks, trenches, breastworks and batteries protecting the beaches. East Anglian examples of these earthworks, especially those at

Great Yarmouth and Weybourne Hope, however have already been published, though more than a generation ago.[1]

The almost general neglect of land defences in the Armada story last year was partly made good in the Greenwich Armada exhibition, and by two articles by Dr Mark Brayshay of the Department of Geographical Sciences, Plymouth Polytechnic. Ian Friel in the Greenwich catalogue[2] compares the respective troop numbers and dispositions of the two sides. The pivotal significance of the camp beyond the Henrician blockhouse of West Tilbury, on the Essex bank of the Thames, strengthened at the last moment by an up-to-date earthwork trace

designed by an Italian military engineer in Elizabeth's pay, Genebelli, was well brought out. With the English government unaware of the projected landing point of the Spanish armies, it was crucial to have the ability to move the field army against either a landing on the Essex coasts or to the beaches of Kent. The blockhouses at West Tilbury and Gravesend covered the ferry across the Thames at this strategic point which would have enabled a flexible English response. The Greenwich exhibition, displaying contemporary charts of the Thames and Medway illustrating their defences, and maps of possible landing places in Kent, demonstrated the extent of some of the defensive preparations. So

[1] B H St J O'Neill, *Castles and Cannon* (Oxford 1960).

[2] M J Rodriguez-Salgado, *et al, Armada 1588 – 1988: An International Exhibition To Commemorate The Spanish Armada*, The Official Catalogue (London 1988).

Mark Brayshay, 'Tudor artillery towers and their role in the defence of Plymouth in 1588', *Devon Historian* 35 (1987), pp3 – 14.

Mark Brayshay, 'Plymouth's Coastal Defences in the Year of the Spanish Armada', *Transactions of the Devonshire Association for the Advancement of Science, Literature and Art* 119 (1987), pp169 – 196

did Edmund Yorke's maps of the East Anglian defences at Great Yarmouth and on the Norfolk coast. Lambarde's map of the beacon system in Kent and examples of the weaponry available to the army and militia completed the summary of local defensive measures.

Mark Brayshay's two papers gave detailed attention to the existing defences at Plymouth, and the frantic preparations for the Armada emergency. 'Tudor artillery towers and their role in the defence of Plymouth in 1588' appeared in the *Devon Historian* of 1987. It makes effective use of five sixteenth century maps to define the positions and form of the five Henrician blockhouses on the waterfront from Plymouth Hoe in the east to Millbay, Firestone Bay and Stonehouse. He includes the later blockhouse at Barnpool at Mount Edgecumbe, and the fortifications on St Nicholas (Drake's) Island, and makes observations on such as remain today.

The second paper, 'Plymouth's Coastal Defences in the Year of the Spanish Armada', appeared a little later in the *Transactions of the Devonshire Association*. This covers contemporary defence plan-

ning more widely and in greater detail. Brayshay makes a fundamental observation when he says: 'The true extent of defence measures taken at the local level in the face of the Armada threat can only be gauged effectively by examining local records and matching them wherever possible with the evidence of national policy making as it is revealed in the State Papers.' Plymouth is fortunate in possessing a range of Borough records as well as the cartographic sources already mentioned. These provide detailed accounts for the repair of the existing bulwarks and for the new emergency works, the provision of a constant watch and for the relaying of information, and the buying and borrowing of ordnance.

The probability that the enhanced defences of Plymouth and the Sound would have proved quickly ineffective had the Armada turned to attack and land its main forces here, applies equally to the country as a whole. Yet it is clear that there would have been resistance, and it is the evidence for such defensive measures that need to be appreciated when the more dramatic naval story of the Armada is retold.

Andrew Saunders

Book Review

M W THOMPSON, *The Decline of the Castle*, published by Cambridge University Press, Cambridge, 1987.
245 × 180mm, viii + 212 pages, 114 illustrations.
ISBN 0 521 32194 8. £15.00

Archaeologists, like most people, are usually more cheerful in considering beginnings than endings, origins than declines; so the title of this book, and some of its chapter headings ('nostalgia', 'accelerating decay', 'destruction') might be thought to be dispiriting. And there are problems of definition. If castles are defined, as they usually are, as the defended residences of feudal lords, they can only truly be called castles while they are fulfilling this role. After that, they are redundant buildings, ancient monuments, romantic

ruins, or, in our own day, 'heritage resource material with tourist potential'. If the idea of the castle, and more importantly its inherent status, but not the fabric, survives, it re-emerges as a skeuomorphological element in country houses, bishop's palaces, or gracing the entrances to Cambridge colleges.

The story, from castles-in-use to castles-in-care, via the Beachy Head of castles-in-the-mind, is a complex and interesting one, and no-one is better qualified than Dr Thompson to tell it. He has

drawn on almost the whole compass of large-scale, late and post-medieval secular architecture, in charting the castle's authentic death-throes, and its post-mortem reverberations, and he takes us to France, Scotland, Ireland, as well as to England and Wales, to do it.

The chronology of decline is not a linear one, and many castles which had been to all intents and purposes abandoned, could be refortified at need, as happened in the Civil War and at other times. The *idea* of the castle lingered on in many forms, in the design of country houses, in the remarkable durability of the Great Tower and the gatehouse, and in non-functional decorative motifs which gave a romantic and embattled air to the country seats of gentlemen. As Thompson says, 'this book is about the house trying to escape from the prison of the castle.' Perhaps the title might have reflected this dualism of approach better, for we hear quite as much about the house as we do about the castle. Indeed, the book is essential reading for students of the origins of our great mansions.

The perambulations of John Leland in the early sixteenth century provide an important commentary on the contemporary condition of castles, and a useful appendix lists his comments, where these are helpful. It is difficult material to interpret, as Thompson points out. Leland is laconic and ambiguous, and one does

not always know what he means, or what we ought to gather, by his terminology. To categorise Leland's assessments under the headings 'normal use', 'partly derelict', and 'ruin', as Thompson does, is probably unwise. What Leland sees as 'normal use' may be very different from what we might think the normal use of a castle is. Often he must have seen merely an elderly monument with 'modern' domestic buildings in it. Still more dangerous is the attempt to quantify the same evidence regionally, at least with divisions so crude as to place Lincolnshire in the same category as the Marches of Wales. A distribution map would have been better. The conclusions which are drawn from this statistical exercise owe more, I hope and believe, to Thompson's experiences and judgment, than to his shaky methodology.

The book is nicely produced, reasonably priced, copiously illustrated with excellent line drawings, and rather darkish photographs. There are one or two errors of fact, deriving from faulty proof-reading, and the style, peppered with exclamation marks, is sometimes ponderous, with occasional ambiguities. But these are minor quibbles. Thompson has done a thorough and interesting job. This reviewer enjoyed the book and warmly recommends it to both general reader and specialist alike.

C M Mahany

Book Review

ROGER WILLOCK, *Bulwark of Empire: Bermuda's Fortified Naval Base 1860–1920*, published by Bermuda Maritime Museum Press, second edition 1988.
xxx + 160 pages, 15 plates, 2 maps. ISBN 0 921560 00 1. Available from Fortress Book Service at £15.00 including p&p.

The rediscovery of Bermuda's remarkable sequence of fortifications, and the unflagging efforts of the Bermuda Maritime Museum to make their importance in the island's his-

tory, and to the study of military engineering in general, more widely known, have been considerable achievements in recent years. It is very much to the Museum's credit that it has published a second edition of this personal and very readable account of Bermuda's nineteenth and twentieth century defences by a US Marine Corps officer who is also a distinguished military historian. This book, privately published at Princeton, New Jersey, in 1962, was the first to be devoted to Bermuda's fortifications.

The reader should not expect an individually detailed and analytical description of the many forts on the islands. That can increasingly be found elsewhere. Its value lies rather in its assessment of the strategic importance of the islands, particularly after American independence, and their place in nineteenth century British colonial defence policy as a whole and as part of a chain of British strategic outposts. The fortifications are therefore seen within this wider context as well as more narrowly in the topography of the islands and the dockyard. As an American it is probably easier for Willock to provide this masterly overview based as it is on Parliamentary papers as well as secondary sources and references to *Brassey's Naval Annual*.

This same broad assessment is applied to the conduct of naval policy, and the role of the North American and West Indies squadron. The development of the dockyard for ship repair and maintenance was the vital element in keeping a naval presence in the western Atlantic. As warships grew even larger, with the coming of steam power, thicker armour and heavier weapons, there was a subsequent requirement for floating docks to keep these facilities up to date. The development of rifled, breech loading guns is also well covered by Willock, especially that in the United States, associated with Dahlgren, Rodman and Parrott.

As a marine colonel and an enthusiast for the 'Blue Water' school of defensive thinking, Willock is more sceptical of the worth of the high level of British expenditure on the nineteenth century fortifications. It is interesting, however, to see how the main weight of Bermuda fortress construction followed immediately upon the massive building campaign in the United Kingdom, which resulted from the recommendations of the Royal Commission on Defence in 1860. The same master-mind lay behind the thinking and design of both sets of fortifications: the assistant Inspector General of Fortifications, William Drummond Jervoise.

For a broad appreciation of British colonial defence policy and as an introduction to the defences of Bermuda this book can scarcely be bettered.

Andrew Saunders

Book Review

ROBERT W EDWARDS, *The Fortifications of Armenian Cilicia*, published by Dumbarton Oaks, Washington DC, 1987 280 × 215mm, xxxii + 288 pages, 302 plate pages, 78 line drawings, 569 monochrome and 48 colour photographs. ISBN 0 88402 163 7. Available from Fortress Book Service at £40 including p & p.

When the First Crusade reached south-east Anatolia, its leaders must have been surprised to find a relatively friendly Christian power already established in Cilicia. This was made up of refugee Armenians who, even before the Byzantine disaster at Manzikert in 1071, had been forced from their traditional homeland by a combination of Turkish pressure from the east and aggressive Byzantine foreign policy from the west. Once the rival baronies were consolidated into a state, known as Little or Lesser Armenia, it was to play an important part in the politics of the Crusader principalities. Although at its apogee under Leo (Leon or Levon) II it was accorded the status of kingdom and survived the mainland Frankish states by nearly a century, its borders were never secure, and for most of its existence it was surrounded by potentially hostile neighbours – the Byzantine empire; Seljuk Turks, Danishmendids and other Muslim powers; and the Crusader states of Antioch and Edessa.

This Kingdom of Cilicia – in what is present-day Turkey – has remained virtually unknown to all except a handful of specialists, but the Armenians were great builders and (not surprisingly, given their turbulent history) they were expert fortification engineers. The strength of the kingdom lay in the Taurus mountains, which even today are inhospitable to wheeled traffic, but their very remoteness has ensured the survival of a wide range of military works in remarkable condition. Previously, a small selection of the larger and/or more accessible castles have been described, but a magnificent new book by the American scholar Robert W Edwards makes a full study of the vast majority of them – 75 in all.

Edwards spent many years of arduous fieldwork in Cilicia, painstakingly surveying the principal sites, most of which were previously unrecorded or unidentified. The catalogue, which forms the core of the book, makes this work available for the first time. Each castle, fortified manor or watchtower is treated to a full archaeological description, combined with a resumé of what little historical information is available for those that can be identified. Most are illustrated with a measured ground plan and a superb portfolio of photographs. Naturally enough, the latter concentrate on archaeological details, but just occasionally the photos hint at the spectacular settings of so many of the mountain strongholds. If any criticism can be made of this section, it is that Edwards' directions on access are often so sketchy that one wonders if he wants to keep these wonderful discoveries to himself! On a more practical level, the road system of southern Turkey has changed so much since he was working in the mid-1970s that his notes on how to find the more obscure sites can be very misleading – one, for example, is now at the bottom of a newly created reservoir.

The catalogue is prefaced by a substantial Introduction that summarises the historical background and, more importantly, sets out twenty distinctive features of Armenian fortification, in terms of design and architecture. He also includes sections on Armenian masonry, on Arab, Byzantine and Crusader military structures in Cilicia, and attempts an outline chronology of surviving fortifications. Like all generalisations his conclusions sound a little too neat, but the evidence is convincingly marshalled in the catalogue. This, then, is a highly important piece of work, allowing for the first time real differentiation on archaeological grounds between Armenian structures and those of other builders, which may make possible the future identification of other sites of historical significance for this poorly documented kingdom.

The Introduction concludes with an essay on the role of military architecture in medieval Cilicia, as part of what the author terms a 'non-urban strategy'; this is so interesting that one longs for more analysis – particularly of the military features and tactical employment of the castles themselves. Nevertheless, in total, the achievement is very impressive and does full justice to some of the finest military structures of the medieval world, hitherto confined to quite undeserving obscurity. In an intriguing aside, Edwards mentions that in the vexed question of local influences on Crusader castle-builders, he believes that Armenian expertise has been greatly undervalued. His future work in Armenia proper will concentrate on the continuity of the Armenian architectural tradition from classical times, and the significance of this in the field of fortification may well produce another work of great importance some years hence.

Robert Gardiner

Books and monographs

PETER FURTADO, et al, *Ordnance Survey Guide to Castles in Britain*, published by Hamlyn/Ordnance Survey (London, new edition 1988).
256 pages, 120 colour illustrations.
ISBN 0 600 55869 X (paper)
0 319 00150 4.
£6.95.

E J GRIMSLEY, *The Historical Development of the Martello Tower in The Channel Islands*, Sarnian Publications (Guernsey 1988).
96 pages, 94 line drawings.
ISBN 0 9513868 0 8
£6.50
The first comprehensive review of the Channel Island gun-towers which mostly ante-date the English Martello towers of the south and east coasts. The associated small forts and batteries are also included in the survey and comparisons are drawn with English works.

D J CATHCART KING, *The Castle in England and Wales: An Interpretative History*, Croom Helm (Beckenham, Kent 1988).
210 pages, 25 line drawings, 9 photos.
ISBN 0 7099 4829 8.
£25.00.
To be reviewed in a future issue.

T E LAWRENCE, *Crusader Castles* (a new edition with introduction and notes by Denys Pringle), published by Oxford University Press, (Oxford 1988).
xl + 154 pages, 108 photos, line drawings, 2 maps.
ISBN 0 19 822964 X.
£30.00
This new edition reproduces the original text without alteration and includes a selection of the pencilled notes in the form of footnotes, which Lawrence added to the typescript in preparation for a revision that was never made. Denys Pringle's introduction reassesses Lawrence's thesis on the influence of the Crusades on western military technology.

HARTWIG NEUMANN, *Festungsbaukunst und Festungsbautechnik*, published by Bernard & Graefe (Koblenz 1988).
440 pages with numerous line drawings and photos in the text.
ISBN 3 7637 5839 9.
Available from the *Fortress* Book Service (see below) at £55 including p & p.
A broad survey of German fortifications which includes not only that within the present boundaries of the Federal and Democratic Republics but also of former German lands and settlements. The first section contains an exhaustive list of fifteenth to twentieth century works. The second section reviews the development of fortress construction from the first half of the nineteenth century through to the present day with particular reference to the New German System as well as to the constructions of the two world wars.

DEREK RENN, *Framlingham and Orford Castles*, official souvenir guide, published by English Heritage (London 1988).
36 pages, illustrated.
ISBN 1 85074 186 7 (paper).
£1.50

RUDI ROLF and PETER SAAL, *Fortress Europe*, first English language edition translated from the Dutch (1986), published by Airlife Publishing Ltd (Shrewsbury 1988).
166 pages, 152 illustrations.
ISBN 0 906393 96 5 (case)
1 85310 032 3 (paper)
£10.95.
The first part of the book summarises the development of military engineering in Europe from 1870 through to the Second World War, with special attention to the German works of the Atlantic Wall. The second and larger part is a guide, country by country, to the surviving works along the coast of Western Europe and on the border between France and Germany.

ROGER F SARTY, *Coast Artillery 1815–1914*, Historical Arms Series, 21, published by Museum Restoration Service (Alexandria Bay, NY, USA 13607–0070 & Bloomfield, Ontario, Canada K0K 1G0 1988).
48 pages illustrated.
ISBN 0 919316 21 2.
[no price quoted]

As well as illustrating British and American coast artillery this booklet contrasts the development of the respective coast defence systems.

ROGER WILLOCK, *Bulwark of Empire: Bermuda's Fortified Naval Base 1860–1920*.
Reviewed in this issue.

Periodical Literature

Fort: The International Journal of Fortification and Military Architecture 16 (1988).

W F K ENGELBRECHT, 'A bastioned entrenchment in Holland'.

GIANNI PERBELLINI, 'The Venetian defences of Cyprus'.

JOHN R KENYON, 'The state of the fortifications in the West Country in 1623'.

ALAIN SALAMANGE, 'Fortifications du XVIIe siècle dans le nord de la France'.

DAVID EVANS, 'The Duke of Richmond, James Glenie, Maker and the Fortifications Bill'.

JOHN E GOODWIN, 'Fortifications against a French invasion of the East Kent coast of England: 1750–1815'.

MAC EOIN BISSET, 'Coast artillery in South Africa: 1899–1955'.

RUDI ROLF, 'Revolving concrete turrets'.

TERRY GANDER, 'The explosive attack on Fort Eben-Emael'.

PAUL AUSTIN, 'Burgh-by-Sands' [stone base for turf sector of Hadrian's Wall], *Current Archaeology* 10 (1988), pp18–19.

JIM CROW, 'Peel Gap' [newly discovered tower on Hadrian's Wall], *Current Archaeology* 10 (1988), pp14–17.

B HARBOTTLE, R FRASER and F C BURTON, 'The Westgate Road Milecastle, Newcastle upon Tyne', *Britannia* XIX (1988), pp153–162.

RICHARD HODGES, 'Origins of the English castle', *Nature* 333 (London 1988), pp112–13.

JOHN REID, 'Niddry Castle revisited', *Archaeology Today* 9(3) (1988), pp38–45, illustrated.

DEREK RENN, 'Hen Domen compared: the evidence for wooden castle buildings in Britain and Normandy', in *From Roman town to Norman castle: essays in honour of Philip Barker* (ed A Burl), published by University of Birmingham Department of Extra-Mural Studies (1988), viii + 86 pages, illustrated.
ISBN 0 7044 0939 9. **£3.50.**

C V WALTHEW, 'Length-units in Roman military planning: Inchtuthil and Colchester', *Oxford Journal of Archaeology* 7 (1988), pp81–98.